Collins
Language
Revolution!
This Time
You'll Remember

# French
## Word Power

**Tony Buzan**
and **Sophie Gavrois**

**Collins**

**First published 2009 by Collins,**
an imprint of HarperCollins Publishers
77-85 Fulham Palace Road
London W6 8JB

**www.collinslanguage.com**

10 9 8 7 6 5 4 3 2 1 0

© HarperCollins Publishers 2009

Mind Map® is a registered trademark of
The Buzan Organisation Ltd and is being
used under licence

ISBN 978-0-00-730219-2

Collins® is a registered trademark of
HarperCollins Publishers Limited

A catalogue record for this book is
available from the British Library

Edited by Cambridge Editorial
Partnership Ltd (www.camedit.com)

Design by Q2AMedia

Printed in Austria by Sony DADC

# Contents

# How to use this book

Congratulations! You are on the road to a fun and easy way to increase your French vocabulary.

This book is based on the principles of **ASSOCIATION, IMAGINATION AND MIND-MAPPING.**

**We remember best when we associate what we learn with something we already know.**

We have divided French words into three "traffic light" categories:

GREEN: the same or nearly the same in English and in French.

Example: *information* is information.

**Green**
for go ahead

The good news is that literally thousands of words are either exactly the same or very similar in the two languages.

**AMBER:** not necessarily the same as the English word, but these words may remind us of another in English that is similar.

Example: the French for *advice* is **conseil**, which looks like the English word "counsel". If you go for counselling, you are going for good advice.

**Amber**
for wait
and think

With amber words, slow down and use the link we suggest between French and something you already know in English.

**RED:** Stop and think! These words may have nothing in common with their English equivalents, but you can remember them by finding a funny (and memorable!) association, playing with the sound of the French word to see if it resembles a word or phrase in English.

**Red**
for stop, think,
make a link

Example: There is a French word that means something between information and advice – **renseignements**. Do you know anyone called Ron? Try to visualise yourself saying to him "Ron, send your mom!" in a strange or ludicrous situation where some kind of help or advice is needed. The more bizarre, funny or even vulgar the situation, the better you'll remember it!

This technique is more fun than learning by rote and much more efficient. It makes languages "un-foreign" by turning foreign words into something that sounds familiar.

## Mind Maps
Mind Maps are one of the best thinking tools available. Some Mind Maps are already drawn for you to help you visualise and retain new information, but the best Mind Maps are those you make yourself. Feel free to add new

branches to the Mind Maps in the book as you increase your vocabulary or make a new Mind Map® with words important to you.

To make a Mind Map® follow these simple steps:

Step one:
Take a blank piece of paper and some coloured pens. Turn the page to landscape format, to make a wide rectangle. In the middle, draw an image of what your Mind Map® is about: for example, if it is about food, draw something delicious.

Step two:
Next draw branches coming out in all directions from your central image, one for each main group of words.

Step three:
Connect second-level branches to the first, and third-level branches to those. Make your branches curves rather than straight lines and use colours and images throughout.

Go to www.collinslanguage.com/revolution to find out more about Mind Mapping.

**Using the book, the CD and the website**
The book is accompanied by a CD, which is crucial. Nobody ever learnt to speak just by reading a book. The CD will help you to get your pronunciation right and to develop your ear and learn to understand spoken French quickly.

You can visit www.collinslanguage.com/revolution for lots of extra interactive exercises. The website also contains answers to the exercises in the book and transcripts for all the recordings.

Schedule some study time (a little every day is much better than several hours once a week) where you can sit down with the book and CD.

## Unité un
# Nourriture et boissons

## Quelque chose à boire   Something to drink

**Green**
for go ahead

Listen to the green words being pronounced and repeat them. As you say each name, visualise the drink.

un **apéritif**  an aperitif
une **bière**  a beer
un **cappuccino**  a cappuccino
un **Coca-Cola®**  a Coke®
un **cocktail**  a cocktail
une **crêpe**  a pancake
un **expresso**  an espresso
un **thé**  a tea
un **whisky**  a whisky

un **café crème**  a white coffee
un **chocolat chaud**  a hot chocolate
un **chocolat viennois**  a hot chocolate with cream
un **digestif**  a liqueur
une **eau minérale**  a mineral water
une **infusion**  a herbal tea
un **vin blanc**  a white wine
un **vin rouge**  a red wine

**Amber**
for wait
and think

Listen to the amber and red words being pronounced and repeat them, visualising your links and images as you do.

### How to remember amber words:

| | |
|---|---|
| **digestif** | think of having a liqueur to help you *digest* a big meal |
| **eau** | think of *eau de cologne*, a liquid that you shouldn't drink! |
| **infusion** | think of herbal tea, which you leave to *infuse* |
| **vin** | think of *vine*, where grapes grow |

**Red**
for stop, think,
make a link

un jus de fruit  a fruit juice
un jus d'orange  an orange juice
un jus de pomme  an apple juice
un jus d'ananas  a pineapple juice
le lait  milk

**To help you memorise red words:**

| | |
|---|---|
| **jus de fruit** | imagine a boy called *Jude* drinking fruit juice–*Jude fruit* |
| **jus de pomme** | imagine *Jude* drinking apple juice wearing a *pom*pom hat–*Jude pom* |
| **jus d'ananas** | imagine *Jude* drinking pineapple juice while riding *on an ass* |
| **lait** | think of Cleopatra *lay*ing down in a bath of ass's milk |

## Activités de mémorisation
Memorising activities

**1. Match the pictures to the names:**

a       b       c       d       e       f       g       h

1.  un vin rouge        4.  un jus d'orange        7.  un thé

2.  une bière           5.  un café                8.  une eau minérale

3.  un cappuccino       6.  un Coca-Cola®

**2. Complete the following names of drinks using one of the endings in the box.**

-tif (x2)   -esso   -anc   -sion   -lat   -me   -nas   -ttes

1. un jus d'ana-
2. un choco-
3. un expr-
4. un diges-
5. un jus de pom-
6. un apéri-
7. un jus de caro-
8. une infu-
9. un vin bl-

**3. Solve these anagrams to find the names of drinks:**

1. NIV CLANB
2. FEAC RECEM
3. ERIBE
4. UEA

**4. Complete with the names of four black drinks:**

1. __ __   __ __ __ __ __ __ __ __

2. __ __   __ __ __ __ __ __ __ __

3. __ __   __ __ __ __ - __ __ __ __

4. __ __   __ __ __ __

**5. Complete with the names of five drinks you can have with milk or cream:**

1. __ __   __ __ __ __   __ __ __ __ __

2. __ __   __ __ __ __ __ __ __   __ __ __ __ __ __ __ __

3. __ __   __ __ __

4. __ __  __ __ __ __ __ __ __ __ __ __ __

5. __ __  __ __ __ __ __ __ __ __ __  __ __ __ __ __ __

**6. Say the word and write it under the pictures:**

a ...........................  b ...........................  c ...........................

d ...........................  e ...........................  f ...........................

**Green**
for go ahead

 **03**

Listen to the green words being pronounced and repeat them. As you do it, visualise the food.

## Quelque chose à manger  Something to eat

**une brioche** a brioche
**le chocolat** chocolate
**la crème** cream
**un croissant** a croissant
**le fruit** fruit
**le gruyère** gruyere cheese
**la mayonnaise** mayonnaise
**une olive** an olive
**une pizza** a pizza
**la salade** salad

le sandwich  a sandwich
le saumon  salmon
une tartine  a slice of bread (with something spread on it)
le thon  tuna
une tomate  a tomato
la vanille  vanilla

un champignon  a mushroom
les chips (f.)  crisps
le croque-monsieur  a toasted ham and cheese sandwich
les frites (f.)  chips
les légumes (m.)  vegetables
le saucisson  salami
un yaourt  a yoghurt

**Amber**
for wait
and think

 o4

Listen to the
amber and red
words being
pronounced and
repeat them,
visualising your
links and images
as you do.

## How to remember amber words:

| | |
|---|---|
| **champignon** | think of the *Champ Union*, where the world mushroom-eating champion is a member |
| **frites** | *free tea* with every portion of chips! |
| **légumes** | think of eating *legumes* in a vegetarian restaurant |

le citron  lemon
la confiture  jam
le fromage  cheese
la glace  ice cream
le jambon  ham
le pain  bread

**Red**
for stop, think,
make a link

## To help you memorise red words:

| | |
|---|---|
| **citron** | think of repelling mosquitoes with a yellow *citronella* candle |
| **confiture** | think of sitting in *comfy tiered* seats at a match and eating a jam sandwich |

| | |
|---|---|
| **fromage** | think of getting a parcel of cheese through the post *from Madge!* |
| **glace** | think of eating the *glacé* cherries off the top of a delicious ice cream |
| **jambon** | imagine you're stuck in a traffic *jam* near a *bon*fire and you're eating ham in your car |
| **pain** | imagine a *pan* full of bread being taken out of the oven |

## Activités de mémorisation
## Memorising activities

**7. A messy menu: tidy up this menu, separating the food from the drinks. List the words in alphabetical order under the headings below:**

cocktail   apéritif   pain   brioche   café   digestif   thé   pizza   frites thon   saucisson   lait   olive   fruits   jus de pomme   bière   confiture gruyère   tartine   eau   vin blanc   champignons   légumes   jambon cappuccino   yaourt   citron   crêpe   saumon   chocolat chaud expresso   mayonnaise   infusion   glace   tomate

**Nourriture:**                **Boisson:**

...............................          ...............................
...............................          ...............................
...............................          ...............................
...............................          ...............................
...............................          ...............................
...............................          ...............................
...............................          ...............................
...............................          ...............................
...............................          ...............................
...............................          ...............................
...............................          ...............................

**8. Match each beginning with the correct ending to make words for items of food:**

| Beginnings | Endings |
|---|---|
| tar | umes |
| champ | mon |
| jam | che |
| piz | sson |
| pa | ture |
| fro | tine |
| crê | za |
| lég | ade |
| gla | ère |
| sau | in |
| confi | mage |
| brio | pe |
| sauci | ignon |
| sal | ce |
| van | ille |
| gruy | bon |

**9. Complete the following words for items of food:**

1. L __ __ __ __ M __ __

2. T __ __ T __ __ __ __

3. F __ __ T __ __ __

4. C __ __ F __ T __ __ __ __

**10. Complete with three words for meat or fish:**

1. J __ __ __ __ __

2. T __ __ __ __

3. S __ __ __ __ __ __

**11. Complete with three food items you might find on a pizza:**

1. F __ __ __ __ __ __

2. T __ __ __ __ __

3. C __ __ __ __ __ __ __ __ __

**12. Say the word and write it under the pictures:**

1 .....................     2 .....................     3 .....................

4 .....................     5 .....................     6 .....................

 05    **13. Mini-dialogues: fill in the missing words, then listen to check:**

**1.** – Bonjour. Qu'est-ce que vous désirez comme boissons?
– (an apple juice and a hot chocolate), s'il vous plaît.
– Vous désirez manger?
– Oui, (a croissant and a toasted ham and cheese sandwich),
s'il vous plaît.
– Très bien.

**2.** – Bonjour. Vous désirez?
– (a herbal tea and an aperitif), s'il vous plaît.
– Vous désirez manger?
– (a yogurt and a pizza), s'il vous plaît.
– Très bien.

## Allons un peu plus loin
### Let's go a bit further

The words learnt in this unit can be combined in many different ways using
**à / à la / au / aux**, to make more precise and complex expressions, like:

**un thé au lait**  tea with milk
**un thé au citron**  tea with lemon
**un cocktail aux fruits**  a fruit-flavoured cocktail
**une glace au café**  a coffee ice cream
**une glace à la vanille**  a vanilla ice cream
**un sandwich au jambon** a ham sandwich
**une brioche au chocolat**  a brioche with chocolate
**un yaourt à la vanille** a vanilla-flavoured yoghurt
**une crêpe à la confiture**  a pancake with jam

**14. Give the English for the following:**

1.  un sandwich au fromage
2.  une pizza aux champignons
3.  un sandwich au thon
4.  un yaourt  aux fruits

**15. Make as many combinations as you can, using the items below:**

crème – chocolat – confiture – fruits – vanille – citron – jambon –
fromage – saumon – gruyère – thon – champignons – saucisson

1.  un sandwich...
2.  une glace...
3.  une pizza...
4.  une crêpe...

If you can't remember the correct linking word, you can always not use it, especially when there are several ingredients or flavours. Café staff are used to quick-fire orders at peak hours!

**un sandwich jambon-fromage**
**une glace vanille-chocolat**
**une pizza jambon champignons**

 o6

**16. What are Charlotte, Aude and Paul ordering? Listen to the dialogue and fill in the missing parts:**

Serveur :    Bonsoir, vous désirez?
Charlotte :  Alors, tout d'abord quelque chose à manger: pour moi ..........
             ..............................................................,
             .......................... et des ...................Et pour toi, Aude?

Aude :       Alors pour moi .............................................................
             et ........................ Et toi, Paul?
Paul :       Ah, pour moi ................................. – ...................
Serveur :    Très bien, et comme boissons?
Charlotte :  Pour moi et Aude .................................., et pour Paul ..............

**17. Order in French:**

1. a ham sandwich
2. a ham salad
3. a ham and tomato sandwich
4. a pancake with chocolate and cream
5. a pizza with mushrooms and tuna

**18. Make up your favourite combinations!**

check your answers at
www.collinslanguage.com/revolution

# Lieux et moyens de transport

With place names, the word for "at" or "to" can be **à**, **au**, **à la**, **à l'**, **aux** or **dans**. The use is idiomatic, so it is better to learn the word with its correct French preposition. First we will look at the words that are followed by **au**, **à la**, **à l'**, and **aux**, then we'll look at those followed by **dans**. Lastly, we'll look at how to get to all these places.

## Lieux Places (1)

**Green**
for go ahead

 07

Listen to the green words being pronounced and repeat them. As you do it, visualise the place

l'aéroport (m.), à l'aéroport  the airport, to/at the airport
la banque, à la banque  the bank, to/at the bank
le bureau, au bureau  the office, to/at the office
le café, au café  the café, to/at the café
le café internet, au café internet  internet café, at the internet café
le château, au château  the castle, to/at the castle
le cinéma, au cinéma  the cinema, to/at the cinema
le concert, au concert  the concert, to/at the concert
- l'entrée (f.), à l'entrée  the entrance, at the entrance
la galerie d'art, à la galerie d'art  the art gallery, to/at the art gallery
le garage, au garage  the (car repair) garage, to/at the garage
l'hôpital (m.), à l'hôpital  the hospital, to/at the hospital
l'hôtel (m.), à l'hôtel  the hotel, to/at the hotel
la maison, à la maison  the house, (going)/at home
le (super)marché, au (super)marché
    the (super)market, to/at the (super)market
la montagne, à la montagne  the mountains, to/in the mountains
le musée, au musée  the museum, to/at the museum
l'office du tourisme (m.), à l'office du tourisme
    the tourist office, to/at the tourist office
le parking, au parking  the car park, to/in the car park
la pharmacie, à la pharmacie  the chemist's, to/at the chemist's
la réception, à la réception  the reception, to/at the reception
le restaurant, au restaurant  the restaurant, to/at the restaurant
le stade, au stade  the football stadium, to/at the football stadium
la station-service, à la station-service
    the service station, to/at the service station
le théâtre, au théâtre  the theatre, to/at the theatre
les toilettes, aux toilettes  the toilet, to the toilet

**Amber**
for wait
and think

 o8

Listen to the
amber and red
words being
pronounced and
repeat them,
visualising your
links and images
as you do.

**le distributeur, au distributeur** the cash machine, ATM, to/at
the ATM
**la mer, à la mer** the seaside, to/at the seaside
**le travail, au travail** work, to/at work

### How to remember amber words:

| | |
|---|---|
| **distributeur** | this is short for **distributeur de billets de banque**, "bank note distributor". Imagine the cash machine as a "money *distributor*", **un distributeur** |
| **mer** | think of *merry* – days by the seaside are usually merry days! |
| **travail** | this sounds a bit like *travel*. Some people prefer to travel instead of going to work! |

**Red**
for stop, think,
make a link

**la campagne, à la campagne** the countryside, in/to the countryside
**l'école (f.), à l'école** the school, to/at school
**la gare, à la gare** the station, to/at the station
**la piscine, à la piscine** the swimming-pool, at/to the swimming-pool

### To help you memorise red words:

| | |
|---|---|
| **campagne** | think of running a *campaign* for the countryside! |
| **école** | imagine a group of *eco*logists who have opened their own school |
| **gare** | think of getting onto the train at Trafal*gar* station |

### Don't forget! Names of cities and towns are preceded by à most of the time:
Je travaille à Paris, J'habite à Londres, Je vais en vacances à Montréal.

**au** is a combination of **à + le**, so it precedes most masculine words.
**à la (à + la)** goes before feminine words.
**à l' (à + l')** goes before words beginning with a vowel or an "h" (masculine or feminine).
**aux (à + les)** goes before masculine and feminine words that are plural.

## Activités de mémorisation
Memorising activities

**1. au, à l', or à la? Put the words below into the right column, depending on whether they go with au, à l', à la or aux. List the words in alphabetical order under the appropriate heading:**

musée  aéroport  réception  gare  office du tourisme  montagne  cinéma  hôtel  galerie  distributeur  supermarché  hôpital  toilettes  mer  parking  parc  château  café  travail  garage  concert  café internet  école  restaurant  station-service

| au: | à l': | à la: | aux: |
|---|---|---|---|
| ............... | ............... | ............... | ............... |
| ............... | ............... | ............... | |
| ............... | ............... | ............... | |
| ............... | ............... | ............... | |
| ............... | ............... | ............... | |
| ............... | ............... | | |
| ............... | | | |
| ............... | | | |
| ............... | | | |
| ............... | | | |
| ............... | | | |

**2. Complete the following names of places using one of the endings below:**

-tion    -re    -son    -teau    -le    -vice    -de

1. à l'éco-
2. au châ-
3. à la sta- -ser-
4. à la ga-
5. à la mai-
6. au sta-

### 3. Où allez-vous? Answer by solving these anagrams:

1. UA MINACE
2. UA NAETRATSUR
3. AAL EGAR
4. UA TIBRUISTURED

### 4. Où se garer? Name four places where you can leave your car:

1. __ __ __ __ __ __ __ __ __ __ __ __ __

2. __ __ __ __ __ __ __ __ __ __ __

3. __ __ __ __ __ __ __ __ __ __ __ __ - __ __ __ __ __ __ __ __ __

4. __ __ __ __ __ __ __ __ __

### 5. Je voudrais aller .... Fill in the blanks with the names of five places where you have to buy a ticket to get in:

1. __ __ __ __ __ __ __ __ __ __

2. __ __ __ __ __ __ __

3. __ __ __ __ __ __ __

4. __ __ __ __ __ __ __

5. __ __ __ __ __ __ __ __ __ __ __ __ __

### 6. Où êtes-vous? Say where you are and write it under the pictures:

a ............................. b ............................. c .............................

d ........................... e ........................... f ...........................

g ...........................

**Green**
for go ahead

 **09**

Listen to the green words being pronounced and repeat them. As you do it, visualise the place.

## Lieux Places (2)

**le centre, dans le centre** the (city) centre, to/in the centre
**la cuisine, dans la cuisine** the kitchen, in/to the kitchen
**l'est, dans l'est** the East, in/to the East
**le nord, dans le nord** the North, in/to the North
**l'ouest, dans l'ouest** the West, in/to the West
**le sud, dans le sud** the South, in/to the South
**le village, dans le village** the village, in/to the village

**la chambre, dans la chambre** the bedroom, in/to the bedroom

### How to remember amber words:

**chambre**  think of the *chamber*maid who cleans your hotel bedroom

**Amber**
for wait and think

**la banlieue, dans la banlieue** the suburbs, in/to the suburbs
**le jardin, dans le jardin** the garden, in/to the garden
**la rue, dans la rue** the street, on/to the street
**la salle de bains, dans la salle de bains**
    the bathroom, in/to the bathroom
**la salle à manger, dans la salle à manger**
    the dining room, in/to the dining room
**le séjour, dans le séjour** the sitting-room, in/to the sitting room

**Red**
for stop, think, make a link

### To help you memorise red words:

**salle de bains**  think of *Sal* the dog being *ban*ned from the bathroom for stealing the toilet paper!

**10**

Listen to the amber and red words being pronounced and repeat them, visualising your links and images as you do.

**salle à manger** — think of *Sal* the dog in a *manger*, eating dinner

**séjour** — imagine baby Lind*say* crawling on a *jour*ney around the living-room

**jardin** — imagine some children making a terrible *din* with a *jar* in the garden

**Don't forget! Names of countries ending with an -e in French are always preceded by en, except Mexique, Cambodge, Zaïre, Zimbabwe and Mozambique:**
Je suis en Italie, J'habite en France, Je vais en vacances en Espagne.

**Names of countries ending in other vowels and consonants are usually preceded by au or aux if they are plural:** Je vais au Canada, J'habite aux Etats-Unis, je vais en vacances au Pérou.

## Activités de mémorisation
Memorising activities

**7. Say where you are going by matching the pictures to the places:**

a          b          c          d          e

1. Je vais dans la cuisine.　　2. Je vais dans l'est.
3. Je vais dans la chambre.　　4. Je vais dans la salle de bains
5. Je vais dans la rue.

**8. Match each beginning with the correct ending to make words for places:**

| Beginnings | Endings |
|---|---|
| dans le séj | ue |
| dans la cham | age |
| dans la salle de b | tre |
| dans le cen | din |
| dans le jar | our |
| dans l'ou | ieu |
| dans la cuis | bre |
| dans la banl | ine |
| dans le vill | est |
| dans la r | ains |

**9. Complete with four words for rooms:**

1. D __ __ __ LE __ __ __ __ __ __ __

2. D __ __ __ LA S__ __ __ __ __ D__ __ __ __ __ __ __

3. D __ __ __ LA C__ __ __ __ __ __ __

4. D __ __ __ LA C__ __ __ __ __ __ __ __

 11

**10. Mini-dialogues: fill in the missing words, then listen to check.**

1. - Alors qu'est-ce qu'on fait cet après-midi? On sort?
   - Oui, bonne idée. Pourquoi ne pas aller (to the town centre)? On pourrait aller (to the cinema) et (to the museum).
   - Très bien. Et demain?
   - S'il fait beau, nous pouvons aller (to the countryside).
   - Ah oui, d'accord!

2. - Où est Olivier?
   - Il est (in the kitchen), il prépare le dîner.
   - Et Catherine? Elle est rentrée?
   - Non, elle est encore (at the office).
   - D'accord. Bon, alors je vais mettre la voiture (in the garage).

# Allons un peu plus loin
## Let's go a bit further

**12**

Listen to these words being pronounced and repeat them.

Here are the words for the main means of transport (moyens de transport):

**l'avion (m.)**  aeroplane
**le bus**  bus
**la voiture**  car
**le vélo**  bicycle
**le métro**  underground, tube
**le train**  train
**la moto**  motorcycle
**le car**  coach
**le taxi**  taxi

The word for "by" is **en** with all means of transport, except for **à pied**, on foot, **à vélo**, by bike, and **à moto**, by motorbike:

**en avion, en bus, en voiture, etc.**

The words for places learnt in this unit can be used with those for the means of transport to make more complex sentences, like:

**pour aller à l'école, je prends le bus**  to go to school, I catch the bus
**je vais au travail en train**  I go to work by train
**je vais à la montagne en voiture**  I go to the mountains by car
**nous allons à l'école à pied**  We walk to school (we go on foot)

# Activités de mémorisation
## Memorising activities

**11. Give the English for the following:**

1. Pour aller au bureau, je prends le bus.
2. Je vais au musée à vélo.
3. Pour aller au stade, je ne prends pas la voiture.
4. Je vais au concert à pied.
5. Je vais à la maison à vélo.
6. Je vais à la montagne en train.

**go to**
**www.collinslanguage.com/revolution**
**for extra activities**

## La journée et la semaine The day and the week

**Green**
for go ahead

 13

Listen to the green amber and red words being pronounced and repeat them, visualising your links and images as you do.

**le week-end** the weekend/at the weekend

**l'apres-midi (f.) (m.) de l'après-midi** afternoon, in the afternoon
**le matin, du matin** morning, in the morning
**la nuit, dans la nuit** night, at night
**le soir, du soir** evening/night, in the evening/night

### How to remember amber words:

| | |
|---|---|
| **matin** | think of *matins*, the morning prayers |
| **après-midi** | think of *après-ski* after skiing at the end of the afternoon. *midi* means noon, *après* means after: *after-noon*. |
| **soir** | think of a *soirée*, a party in the evening. |
| **nuit** | imagine someone moaning because you're too noisy: "we work hard during the day *n'we* sleep at night!" |

**Amber**
for wait
and think

**lundi** Monday
**mardi** Tuesday
**mercredi** Wednesday
**jeudi** Thursday
**vendredi** Friday
**samedi** Saturday
**dimanche** Sunday

**Red**
for stop, think,
make a link

**le jour** the day
**la semaine** the week

**To help you memorise red words:**

| | |
|---|---|
| **lundi** | on Monday, you go to *Lundy* Island |
| **mardi** | on Tuesday, you go to the *Mardi* Gras parade |
| **mercredi** | on Wednesday, *Merv*in won't give you any *credit* |
| **jeudi** | on Thursday, you beg the *judge* to "let *Dee* go!" |
| **vendredi** | on Friday, the *vend*ing machine is *ready* |
| **samedi** | on Saturday, you see *Sam* and *Dee* |
| **dimanche** | on Sunday, you hear *Dee munch*ing on an apple |

**Don't forget: the green French names of the days of the week are always written with a small letter.**

## Activités de mémorisation
### Memorising activities

**1. Join the French words on the left to the correct English meaning on the right:**

| | |
|---|---|
| 1. dimanche | a. evening |
| 2. matin | b. Sunday |
| 3. lundi | c. Thursday |
| 4. après-midi | d. Monday |
| 5. vendredi | e. morning |
| 6. jour | f. week |
| 7. mercredi | g. weekend |
| 8. samedi | h. Tuesday |
| 9. nuit | i. Friday |
| 10. mardi | j. Saturday |
| 11 soir | k. day |
| 12. jeudi | l. Wednesday |
| 13. semaine | m. night |
| 14. week-end | n. afternoon |

**2. Complete the following words using one of the beginnings below:**

après    jo    di    mer    sam    ven    ma    sem

1. -aine
2. -midi
3. -manche
4. -tin

5. -ur
6. -credi
7. -dredi
8. -edi

**3. Solve the anagrams of these names of days or parts of the day:**

1. TUNI
2. RISO

3. DULIN
4. DUJIE

**4. Add the missing letters to make four names of days:**

1. __ __ M __ __ __ __ __ __

2. __ __ R __ __

3. __ __ __ __ __ __ I

4. __ __ R __ __ __ __ __ __

**5. Complete with the first four days of the week**

1. __ __ __ __ __ __

2. __ __ __ __ __ __

3. __ __ __ __ __ __ __ __

4. __ __ __ __ __

**6. Say what part of the day it is and write the answer under the picture:**

C'est ...

1 ....................    2 ....................    3 ....................    4 ....................

**7. Join the words you have learnt to say the French for:**

1. Monday morning
2. Saturday evening
3. Friday night

4. Tuesday afternoon
5. Wednesday evening
6. Sunday night

## Mois et saisons Months and seasons

**Green**
for go ahead

mai May
septembre September
octobre October
novembre November
décembre December

 14

Listen to the
green words
being
pronounced and
repeat them.

l'automne autumn

janvier January
février February
mars March
avril April
juin June
juillet July

**Amber**
for wait
and think

### How to remember amber words:

| | |
|---|---|
| **avril** | just one letter is different! |
| **janvier, février, mars, juin, juillet** | the beginnings of these words are very similar to their English equivalents, so just memorise the endings. |

**Red**
for stop, think,
make a link

août August
le printemps spring
l'été (m.) summer
l'hiver (m.) winter

 15

Listen to the
amber and red
words being
pronounced and
repeat them,
visualising your
links and images
as you do.

### To help you memorise red words:

| | |
|---|---|
| **août** [oot] | think that in August you'd like to walk bare*foot* along the beach! |

| | |
|---|---|
| **printemps** | think of *spring time* |
| **été** | in the summer, you'd like a *ta*ble on a *terra*ce |
| **hiver** | it sounds a bit like *fever*, which you might catch in winter |

**Don't forget: the names of months and seasons are also written with small letters in French.**

## Activités de mémorisation
Memorising activities

**8. Put the names of the months and the seasons in their correct chronological order:**

mars   juin   automne   octobre   été   juillet   décembre   février
printemps   janvier   hiver   août   novembre   avril   mai   septembre

**Mois**

1. ..............................
2. ..............................
3. ..............................
4. ..............................
5. ..............................
6. ..............................
7. ..............................
8. ..............................
9. ..............................
10. ..............................
11. ..............................
12. ..............................

**Saisons**

1. ..............................
2. ..............................
3. ..............................
4. ..............................

**9. Match each beginning with the correct ending to make words for months or seasons:**

| Beginnings | Endings |
|---|---|
| print | ier |
| ma | embre |
| nov | emps |
| ju | llet |
| jui | rier |
| av | rs |
| ao | ût |
| janv | in |
| hiv | ril |
| fév | er |

**10. Complete the following names of months:**

1. ___ ___ __l__

2. __ U __ __ __

3. __ O __ __

4. __ __ __ O __ __ __ __

**11. Complete the following names of seasons:**

1. E __ __

2. __ __ __ __ M __ __

3. __ __ __ N __ __ __ __ __ __

4. __ __ __ E __

 16

**12. Mini-dialogues: fill in the missing words, then listen to check:**

1. - Quelle est ta saison préférée?
   - (the summer) bien sûr! Pendant les mois de (June, July) et d'août, il fait beau et ce sont les vacances.
   - C'est vrai, mais (the spring) est aussi une belle saison. En (May) il fait moins froid et tout est en fleurs.

2. - En (January) il a fait très froid cette année.
   - Oui, en France aussi. Nous sommes allés au ski.
   - Nous, nous partons en vacances seulement fin (March).

- Généralement, nous préférons partir en vacances en (autumn), quand il y a moins de monde. Cette année, en (November) nous partons en croisière.

## Allons un peu plus loin
### Let's go a bit further

Here are some useful idiomatic expressions related to the parts of the day:

**17**

Listen to these expressions being pronounced and repeat them.

**ce matin**  this morning
**cet après-midi**  this afternoon
**ce soir**  this evening, tonight
**le matin de bonne heure**  early in the morning
**tard le soir**  in the late evening
**en début d'après-midi**  early in the afternoon
**en fin d'après-midi**  late in the afternoon
**en pleine nuit**  in the dead of night
**une nuit blanche**  sleepless night
**quinze jours**  a fortnight
**chaque jour/semaine/mois**  every day/week/month

**Don't forget:**

**lundi** = on Monday          **le lundi** = on Mondays

**du lundi au vendredi** = from Monday to Friday

**en janvier, en février, etc.** = in January, in February, etc.

**en été, en automne, en hiver** = in the summer, autumn, winter, but **au printemps** = in the spring

**début** + month = at the beginning of + month

Now you can try using some of these expressions with the other words learnt in this unit and in the previous one:

**du lundi au vendredi, je travaille du matin de bonne heure jusqu'en fin d'après-midi** from Monday to Friday I work from early in the morning until late afternoon

**chaque dimanche après-midi, je vais au stade** every Sunday afternoon, I go to the stadium

**début septembre, je vais à la campagne pendant quinze jours** at the beginning of September, I go to the countryside for a fortnight

---

**13. Give the English for the following:**

1. Je regarde la télé tard le soi.r
2. Je n'aime pas les nuits blanches.
3. Je vais au théâtre chaque semaine.
4. Le dimanche soir, je vais au restaurant avec mes amis.

---

**14. Say in French:**

1. Every morning I go to work by bus.
2. This evening I am going to the theatre.
3. In the summer I am going on holiday.
4. On Saturday afternoons I go to the supermarket.
5. In August I'm going to the seaside.

---

**Tony's Tip**

One of the best ways to consolidate language is by making the new words and expressions relevant. Think of your own life and circumstances and make up sentences that are relevant to you and your daily routines, using the expressions you have learnt in this unit.

## Formes et aspect  Shapes and appearance

**Green**
for go ahead

 18

Listen to the
green words being
pronounced and
repeat them. As
you do it, visualise
something in that
size or shape.

**Amber**
for wait
and think

**Red**
for stop, think,
make a link

19

Listen to the
amber and red
words being
pronounced and
repeat them,
visualising your
links and images
as you do.

**long(ue)**  long
**moyen(ne)**  medium
**rectangulaire**  rectangular
**triangulaire**  triangular

**court(e)**  short (in length)
**haut(e)**  tall, high
**large**  wide
**petit(e)**  short (in height)
**profond(e)**  deep
**rond(e)**  round, circular

### How to remember amber words:

| | |
|---|---|
| **petit** | someone who is *petty*-minded doesn't have very lofty thoughts |
| **court** | think of mini-tennis for children, played on a short *court* |
| **haut** | think of *haute couture*, fashion at very high prices! |
| **large** | looks like *large:* a large person is probably quite wide! |
| **profond** | *profound* is another word for deep |
| **rond** | just take the *u* out of *round* and you have the French word |

**carré(e)**  square-shaped
**étroit(e)**  narrow, tight
**gros(se)**  large, big

**To help you memorise red words:**

| | |
|---|---|
| **carré** | think of the writer John le *Carré* writing square books |
| **étroit** | imagine how you have to be *adroit* to get through a narrow space |
| **gros** | think of people who *grow* big |

**Don't forget: many French adjectives ending with a consonant are turned into the feminine form by adding an -e, while many adjectives that end in –e have the same form in the masculine and the feminine.**

**The most frequent questions related to shape and appearance are:**

| | |
|---|---|
| **Quelle forme?** | What shape is it? |
| **C'est comment?** | What is it like? |

## Activités de mémorisation
Memorising activities

**1. Put the adjectives below in to pairs of opposites, according to their meaning and ending:**

long   grand   étroit   court   large   longue   grande   courte   petite
large   étroite   petit

—                                          +

1. ...................................        1. ...................................
2. ...................................        2. ...................................
3. ...................................        3. ...................................
4. ...................................        4. ...................................
5. ...................................        5. ...................................
6. ...................................        6. ...................................

## 2. Complete the following words using one of the beginnings below:

moy    trian    car    rect    pro    ro    pet    étr

1. -it
2. -en
3. -angulaire
4. -oit

5. -gulaire
6. -nd
7. -fond
8. -ré

## 3. Solve the anagrams of these words which describe appearance:

1. ATUH
2. NOGL
3. RALEG
4. TETIP

## 4. Add the missing letters to make four words which describe shape or appearance:

1. ___ ___ O ___ ___ ___ ___

2. ___ ___ ___ D

3. ___ A ___ ___ ___

4. ___ ___ ___ ___ T

## 5. C'est comment? Complete with four words which describe appearance:

1. M ___ ___ ___ ___

2. P ___ ___ ___ ___

3. E ___ ___ ___ ___ ___

4. C ___ ___ ___ ___ ___

**6. Quelle forme? Say and write down the shapes:**

C'est

.....................　.....................　.....................　.....................

**7. Join the expressions you have learnt to say the French for:**

1. Tall and square
2. Short and round
3. Large and deep

4. Long and rectangular
5. Small and triangular

**Green**
for go ahead

 **20**

Listen to the green words being pronounced and repeat them.

# **Dimensions** Size

**le centimètre** centimetre
**le diamètre** diameter
**la dimension** dimension, size
**la distance** distance
**le kilomètre** kilometre
**la largeur** width
**la mesure** measurement, size
**mesurer** to measure
**le mètre** metre

**Amber**
for wait
and think

**la longueur** length
**le mètre carré** square metre
**la profondeur** depth
**la superficie** surface, area

**How to remember amber words:**

**Red**
for stop, think,
make a link

⊙ **21**

Listen to the amber and red words being pronounced and repeat them, visualising your links and images as you do.

**profondeur**　　*profundity* is another word for depth

**superficie**　　think of *superficial*, which is related to surface

**combien?** how much
**la hauteur** height
**quel(le)...?** which, what...?

**To help you memorise red words:**

**combien**       you could think of a *combine* harvester and wonder how much corn it could cut in a day, switch the last two letters of combine and you get **combien**

**quel(le)...?**       you could think of a witch (which) using her witch's hat (w-hat) to *quell* the flames around her cauldron when her spell gets out of hand

**Don't forget: the most frequent questions related to size are:**

**Combien mesure...?**   How big/tall is...?

**Quelle est sa (hauteur/largeur/profondeur/longueur)?**
What is its (height/width/depth/length)?

**Quelle est la distance?**   What is the distance?

## Activités de mémorisation
Memorising activities

**8. Match each French word in the first set with its English equivalent in the second set:**

distance    mesurer    dimension    largeur    longueur    hauteur    mètre centimètre    profondeur    superficie    kilomètre    combien?    quel(le)(?) mètre carré    diamètre

surface    kilometre    square metre    measure    length    height    depth width    how much?    distance    size    metre    centimetre    which? diameter

| French | English |
| --- | --- |
| 1. ............................... | 1. ............................... |
| 2. ............................... | 2. ............................... |
| 3. ............................... | 3. ............................... |
| 4. ............................... | 4. ............................... |

| | |
|---|---|
| 5. .............................. | 5. .............................. |
| 6. .............................. | 6. .............................. |
| 7. .............................. | 7. .............................. |
| 8. .............................. | 8. .............................. |
| 9. .............................. | 9. .............................. |
| 10. .............................. | 10. .............................. |
| 11. .............................. | 11. .............................. |
| 12. .............................. | 12. .............................. |
| 13. .............................. | 13. .............................. |
| 14. .............................. | 14. .............................. |
| 15. .............................. | 15. .............................. |

**9. Match each beginning with its correct ending to make words related to size:**

| Beginnings | Endings |
|---|---|
| ki | sion |
| me | timètre |
| hau | ficie |
| dia | stance |
| dimen | gueur |
| cen | geur |
| super | sure |
| di | fondeur |
| lon | lomètre |
| lar | mètre |
| pro | teur |

**10. Complete the following words which describe sizes:**

1.   __ __ __ T __ __ __

2.   __ __ O __ __ __ __ __ __ __

3.   __ __ P __ __ __ __ __ __ __ __

4.   __ __ A __ __ __ __ __

**11. Complete the following words related to measurements:**

1. C __ __ __ __ __ __ __ __ __ __

2. K __ __ __ M __ __ __ __ __

3. M __ __ __ __ __

4. __ __ __ __ R __ __ __ A __ __ __

 22

**12. Mini-dialogues: fill in the missing words, then listen to check:**

1. – Combien ...... la pièce?
   – Elle mesure six mètres ......, trois mètres de long et deux de .....

2. – Combien ...... la table?
   – Elle mesure un ..... cinquante de long et quatre-vingt centimètres de .........
   – Et quelle est sa hauteur?
   – Elle mesure soixante centimètres ... haut.

## Allons un peu plus loin
Let's go a bit further

**13. Match each French sentence to its English equivalent:**

1. C'est assez petit, cela mesure seulement cinquante centimètres de haut.
2. C'est long et étroit, et cela mesure un mètre vingt de long.
3. C'est rectangulaire et cela mesure quatre-vingts centimètres de large.
4. C'est grand, cela mesure huit mètres carrés.
5. C'est carré, et cela mesure quarante centimètres de profondeur.
6. C'est rond, cela mesure soixante-dix centimètres de diamètre.

a. It's big, it's 8 square metres.
b. It's rather small, only 50 cm high
c. It's square, 40 cm deep
d. It's long and narrow, 1.20 m long

e. It's rectangular, 80 cm wide
f. It's round, 70 cm in diameter

## 14. Match each question to the correct answer:

1. Quelle est la hauteur?
2. Quelle est la longueur?
3. Quel est le diamètre?
4. Quelle est la distance?

5. Quelle est la profondeur?
6. Quelle est la superficie?

7. Quelle est la largeur?
8. C'est comment?

a. Cela mesure quarante-cinq mètres de profondeur.
b. Cela mesure vingt mètres de long.
c. Cela mesure un mètre de haut.
d. Cela mesure soixante-quinze centimètres.
e. Quinze kilomètres.
f. Cela mesure quatre-vingts centimètres de large.
g. C'est petit et étroit.
h. Cela mesure dix mètres carrés.

## 15. Describe the shape, size and appearance of the following objects in French:

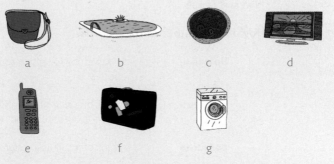

a

b

c

d

e

f

g

**Tony's Tip**

Practise by writing down the shape, size and appearance of a few objects around your house or office on record cards, and writing the name of the object on the reverse of the card. Then put all the cards in a tin and pull a few out every day: see if you can identify the object by its description, or, even better, describe the object again!

**go to**
www.collinslanguage.com/revolution
**for extra activities**

## Vêtements Clothes

**Green**
for go ahead

le bikini Bikini ®
le cardigan cardigan
le jeans jeans
le pyjama pyjamas
le pull(over) sweater
les sandales (f.) sandals
le t-shirt t-shirt

**Amber**
for wait
and think

les bottes (f.) boots
le chapeau hat
le costume man's suit
la cravate tie
l'imperméable (m.) raincoat
le pantalon trousers
la robe dress
la veste jacket

 23

Listen to the
green and amber
words being
pronounced and
repeat them. As
you do say the
word, visualise
the item of
clothing.

### How to remember amber words:

| | |
|---|---|
| **bottes** | swap an 'o' for a 't' in *boots* and you get bottes! |
| **chapeau** | think of a *chap* shouting "*Oh!*" as his hat blows away in the wind |
| **costume** | think of a suit as a *costume* for work |
| **cravate** | think of a *cravat* in the form of a tie |
| **imperméable** | something *impermeable* is water-proof, as a raincoat should be! |
| **pantalon** | remember that Americans call trousers *pants*, or think of the word *pantaloons* |
| **robe** | think of ward*robe*, where a woman keeps her dresses |

**veste**　think of walking out of the house wearing a *vest* over your clothes – then remembering that you should have put on your jacket!

**la ceinture**  belt
**les chaussettes (f.)**  socks
**les chaussures (f.)**  shoes
**la chemise**  shirt
**le chemisier**  blouse
**l'écharpe (f.)**  scarf
**les gants (m.)**  gloves
**la jupe**  skirt
**le manteau**  coat
**les sous-vêtements (m.)**  underwear
**le tailleur**  woman's suit

**Red**
for stop, think, make a link

 24

Listen to the red words being pronounced and repeat them, visualising your links and images as you do.

**To help you memorise red words:**

**ceinture**　think of a belt worn by a Roman *centurion*

**chaussettes**　imagine a footwear fashion *show* where you are given a *set* of socks!

**chaussures**　think of a TV *show* about walking shoes, the kind you feel safe and *sure* wearing

**chemise**　think of your best friend wearing a silver shirt that *shimmers* in the sunlight

**chemisier**　think of a girl wearing a blouse and dancing, saying "the *shimmy* is *easier* than the tango!"

**écharpe**　think of a *sharp*-eyed lady wearing a pretty scarf

**gant**　imagine a knight throwing down the *gaunt*let, his metal glove, challenging you to remember the French word!

**jupe**　imagine a skirt with large red spots that look like the planet *Jup*iter printed on it

| | |
|---|---|
| **manteau** | think of keeping a me*mento* of your first day at work in your coat pocket |
| **sous-vêtements** | link **sous**, which means *under*, and *vestments*, as special clothes you wear under your other clothes |
| **tailleur** | think of a *tailor* who makes women's suits |

**Tony's Tip**

To remember the gender of words for clothes, imagine Napoléon wearing the masculine items and Brigitte Bardot wearing the feminine ones!

## Activités de mémorisation
### Memorising activities

**1. A messy wardrobe. Tidy up the clothes below, listing them in alphabetical order according to two categories: vêtements d'homme (menswear), vêtements de femme (womenswear). If clothes are suitable for both men and women, list them twice.**

costume   imperméable   bikini   pyjama   chemisier   veste   robe
écharpe   chemise   pull   jeans   bottes   ceinture   cardigan
chaussettes   cravate   tailleur   gants   chapeau   sous-vêtements
chaussures   t-shirt   manteau   jupe   sandales   pantalon

| **vêtements d'homme** | **vêtements de femme** |
|---|---|
| 1. ................... | 1. ................... |
| 2. ................... | 2. ................... |
| 3. ................... | 3. ................... |
| 4. ................... | 4. ................... |
| 5. ................... | 5. ................... |
| 6. ................... | 6. ................... |
| 7. ................... | 7. ................... |
| 8. ................... | 8. ................... |

9. .....................
10. .....................
11. .....................
12. .....................
13. .....................
14. .....................
15. .....................
16. .....................
17. .....................
18. .....................
19. .....................
20. .....................
21. .....................

9. .....................
10. .....................
11. .....................
12. .....................
13. .....................
14. .....................
15. .....................
16. .....................
17. .....................
18. .....................
19. .....................
20. .....................
21. .....................
22. .....................
23. .....................

**2. Match each beginning with the correct ending to make words for items of clothing:**

| Beginnings | Endings |
|---|---|
| ve | tume |
| pyj | perméable |
| pan | hirt |
| cos | vate |
| im | dales |
| che | lleur |
| t-s | isier |
| cra | teau |
| chem | ste |
| tai | mise |
| man | ama |
| san | talon |

**3. Solve the anagrams of these words to find the names of footwear or accessories:**

1. RAHEPC
2. TOTEBS

3. UTERENIC
4. EHAPUAC

**4. Add the missing letters to make four words which describe types of tops:**

1. __-__ __ __l__ __ __

3. __ __ __ __ D__ __ __ __ __ __

2. __ __ __L__ __

4. __ __ __S__ __ __

**5. Complete with four words which describe items of clothing that cover most of the body:**

1. R__ __ __ __

4. __A__ __ __ __ __ __

2. __ __ __ __T__ __ __ __

5. __ __ __ __ __ __ __ __R

3. __ __ __ __A__ __ __

**6. Say the word and write it under the pictures:**

a ...............  b ...............  c ...............  d ...............

e ...............  f ...............  g ...............  d ...............

## **Couleurs** Colours

**Green**
for go ahead

**beige** beige
**orange** orange

**blanc/blanche** white
**bleu(e)** blue
**gris(e)** grey

rose  pink
**rouge**  red
**vert(e)**  green
**violet(te)**  purple

**Amber**
for wait
and think

## How to remember amber words:

| | |
|---|---|
| **blanc** | think about a *blank* sheet of paper, which is totally white |
| **bleu** | swap the 'e' and 'u' around in blue and you get the French word |
| **rouge** | think of *rouge*, used to redden the cheeks |
| **rose** | think of *rosy* cheeks |
| **vert** | think of *verdant*, which means bright green |
| **violet** | think of the colour of a *violet* |

**jaune**  yellow
**marron**  brown
**noir(e)**  black

**Red**
for stop, think,
make a link

⊚ 25

Listen to the
green, amber and
red words being
pronounced and
repeat them,
visualising the
colours as you do.

## To help you memorise red words:

| | |
|---|---|
| **jaune** | think of *jaun*dice, a disease which makes the eyes look yellow |
| **marron** | imagine the colour of *mar*mite *on* a slice of toast |
| **noir** | think of *film noir*, crime films with characters who have dark thoughts |

**Don't forget: the most frequent question related to colours is**

**C'est de quelle couleur?**  What colour is it?

## Activité de mémorisation
Memorising activities

**7. Using coloured pencils or felt-tips, write down all the French words for colours in alphabetical order. Then write the equivalent English words in the second list.**

rouge   bleu   noir   gris   rose   jaune   beige   blanc   orange   vert   marron   violet

grey   yellow   pink   blue   brown   purple   orange   green   beige   white   red   black

| Français | English |
|---|---|
| 1. ................. | 1. ................. |
| 2. ................. | 2. ................. |
| 3. ................. | 3. ................. |
| 4. ................. | 4. ................. |
| 5. ................. | 5. ................. |
| 6. ................. | 6. ................. |
| 7. ................. | 7. ................. |
| 8. ................. | 8. ................. |
| 9. ................. | 9. ................. |
| 10. ................. | 10. ................. |
| 11. ................. | 11. ................. |
| 12. ................. | 12. ................. |
| 13. ................. | 13. ................. |

**8. Complete the names of colours using one of the endings below:**

-ise    -une    -ir    -che    -ge    -se    -rt    -let
-nge    -ron    -ge    -eu

1. blan–
2. ro–
3. ja–
4. rou–
5. bl–
6. bei–
7. vio–
8. gr–
9. ora
10. ve–
11. no–
12. mar–

**9. Complete with the colours of earth, a sunflower, coal and lilac:**

1. ___ ___ ___ R ___ ___

3. ___ ___ ___ R

2. ___ A ___ ___ ___

4. ___ ___ ___ L ___ ___

**10. Complete with the colours of the French flag:**

1. ___ ___ E ___

2. ___ ___ A ___ ___

3. ___ ___ U ___ ___

**11. Mini-dialogues: Listen to the dialogues and identify which of the pictures a–g are being referred to:**

26

1: ...................

2: ...................

3: ...................

a          b          c          d          e          f          g

# Allons un peu plus loin
## Let's go a bit further

To increase the variety of colours, you can add **clair**, light, or **foncé**, dark, after the name of a colour. Here are some examples:

**gris clair**  light grey
**vert foncé**  dark green
**rouge foncé**  dark red

**bleu foncé**  dark yellow
**marron clair**  light brown
**bleu clair**  dark blue

**12. C'est de quelle couleur? Say the English equivalent of these colours:**

1. jaune foncé
2. vert clair
3. bleu clair

4. gris foncé
5. rose foncé
6. orange clair

**13. Now try saying these colours in French:**

1. light beige
2. light red
3. dark purple

4. dark brown
5. light pink
6. dark orange

Another possibility is to combine the colour with an item that represents the shade, so **vert pomme** is *apple green*, **jaune citron** is *lemon yellow*, **bleu marine** is *navy blue*, and so on.

**14. Find the English equivalent for these colours. You may need to refer to a dictionary.**

1. rouge tomate
2. gris anthracite
3. jaune canari
4. vert pomme
5. rouge brique
6. vert bouteille

7. rose saumon
8. jaune citron
9. bleu ciel
10. gris perle
11. bleu lavande
12. bleu roi

**15. Describe the clothes in the pictures as fully as you can, following the example. Don't forget to use the words for size and appearance that you learnt in Unit 4!**

# Pour finir: Mind Map it!

Draw a mind map of clothes and colours. Don't forget to add the adjectives for size and appearance from Unit 4.

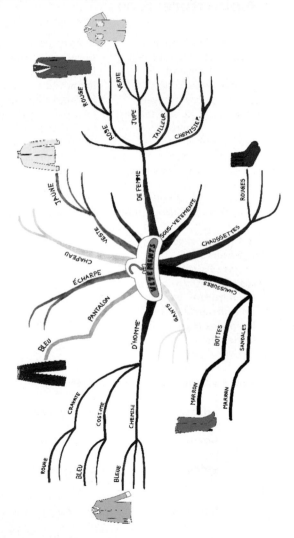

# 6

## Nourriture Food

**Green**
for go ahead

(◎) 27

Listen to the green and amber words being pronounced and repeat them. As you do so, visualise the item of food.

l'asperge (f.) asparagus
l'aubergine (f.) aubergine
la carotte carrot
la côtelette cutlet
la courgette courgette
le dessert dessert
le gratin gratin
les lasagnes lasagne
le melon melon
l'omelette (f.) omelette
les pommes
de terre (f.) potatoes
les petits pois (m.) peas

le porc pork
la ratatouille ratatouille
le risotto risotto
la salade de fruit fruit salad
la salade verte green salad
la sardine sardine
la sauce sauce
le saucisson sausage (the kind you slice)
le saumon salmon
la soupe soup
les spaghettis (m.) spaghetti
la tarte tart
la tomate tomato

**Amber**
for wait
and think

le bifteck steak
le boeuf beef
le gâteau cake
les haricots (m.) beans
les légumes vegetables
l'oignon (m.) onion
les pâtes (f.) pasta
le riz rice
la truite trout

### How to remember amber words:

| | |
|---|---|
| **bifteck** | it's *beef steak* without the 's' |
| **boeuf** | think of eating beef in the *buff* ! |
| **gâteau** | we call some types of cake *"gateau"* in English |
| **haricots** | think of *haricots*, which are a type of bean |

| | |
|---|---|
| **légumes** | think of eating *legumes* in a vegetarian restaurant |
| **oignon** | take *onion*, shake it a bit and add a 'g', you'll get *oignon* |
| **pâtes** | think of *pat*ting some pasta with a spoon |
| **riz** | imagine being *re*-energised by eating some rice! |
| **truite** | some people think that a trout is a *treat*! |

**l'agneau (m.)** lamb
**les champignons (m.)** mushrooms
**les épinards (m.)** spinach
**le foie** liver
**le fromage** cheese
**les fruits de mer (m.)** seafood
**la glace** ice cream
**le jambon** ham
**les oeufs (m.)** eggs
**le poisson** fish
**le poivron** (sweet) pepper
**le poulet** chicken
**le thon** tuna
**la viande** meat

**Red**
for stop, think,
make a link

 28

Listen to the red
words being
pronounced and
repeat them,
visualising your
links and images
as you do.

**To help you memorise red words:**

| | |
|---|---|
| **l'agneau** | Imagine calling your friend *Anne*, "*Yo!*" but she can't hear you because she's out in the fields with the lambs |
| **champignons** | think of the *Champ Union*, where the world mushroom-eating champion is a member |
| **épinards** | François Pienaar was a famous captain of the South African rugby team. Imagine calling him, "*Hey, Pienaar!* Come and get your spinach!" |

| | |
|---|---|
| **foie** | You probably know that *foie* gras is made from goose liver |
| **fromage** | think of getting a parcel of cheese through the post *from Madge*! |
| **fruits de mer** | Remember in Unit 2 you thought of *merry* for *mer*? Now you can think of being merry as you pick seafood from a tree – like fruit!" |
| **glace** | think of eating the *glacé* cherries off the top of a delicious ice cream |
| **jambon** | imagine you're stuck in a traffic *jam* near a *bon*fire and you're eating ham in your car |
| **oeufs** | imagine a *loaf* you are eating with eggs |
| **poisson** | unfortunately you can get food *poisoning* when eating fish |
| **poivron** | imagine eating peas, petits *pois*, with peppers cut in the form of che*vrons* |
| **poulet** | in the *pool, a* chicken cannot swim |
| **thon** | imagine a tuna weighing a *ton* |
| **viande** | imagine you had some very nice meat in South America when you went from Peru to Bolivia *via* the *Andes* |

## Activités de mémorisation
Memorising activities

**1. A messy menu. Tidy up the food below, listing the types of food in alphabetical order according to four categories: entrées (starters), plat principal (main course), divided into meat or fish and side dishes, and desserts. If items are suitable for more than one category, list them twice.**

les carottes    les épinards    le saumon    les lasagnes    le poulet
les fruits de mer    le jambon    le biftteck    la truite    l'agneau
le gâteau    les champignons    la côtelette    la salade    le melon
le riz    le thon    les pommes de terre    les petits pois    les poivrons
la soupe    le bœuf    le foie    les haricots

| entrée | plat principal viandes/poissons garniture | | desserts |
|---|---|---|---|
| 1. ............... | 1. ............... | 1. ............... | 1. ............... |
| 2. ............... | 2. ............... | 2. ............... | |
| 3. ............... | 3. ............... | 3. ............... | |
| 4. ............... | 4. ............... | 4. ............... | |
| 5. ............... | 5. ............... | 5. ............... | |
| 6. ............... | 6. ............... | 6. ............... | |
| 7. ............... | 7. ............... | 7. ............... | |
| | 8. ............... | 8. ............... | |
| | 9. ............... | 9. ............... | |
| | | 10. ............... | |

## 2. Match the pictures to the names of food:

a         b         c         d         e         f         g         h

1. la soupe          2. le poulet          3. le riz
4. le biftteck       5. les spaghettis     6. la côtelette
7. les oeufs         8. la truite

## 3. Solve the anagrams to find types of food:

1. GOREMFA                    3. NOSPISO
2. MEUGELS                    4. SETAP

### 4. Add the missing letters to find four types of meat:

1. __ G__ __ __ __ __

3. __ __ __ __ L __ __ __

2. __ __ R __ __

4. __ __ __ E __ __ __ __ __ E

### 5. Complete with four types of fish:

1. __ __ __ __ __ __ __ __

3. __ __ __ __ __ __ __

2. __ __ __ __ __

4. __ __ __ __ __ __ __

### 6. Say the word and write it under the pictures:

a ..................... b ..................... c ..................... d .....................

## Façons de cuisiner Styles of cooking

As you saw in Unit 1, you can use **au/à la/à l'/aux** etc. to combine words to name a particular food more precisely.

**gâteau au café/au citron** coffee/lemon-flavoured cake
**glace aux fruits** fruit-flavoured ice cream
**gratin aux asperges** asparagus gratin
**tomates à l'huile d'olive** tomatoes with olive oil
**soupe à l'oignon** onion soup

You can also use this construction to indicate the style of cooking.

**à la milanaise** Milanese style
**au barbecue** barbecued
**au grill** cooked on a grill
**bouilli(e)** boiled
**braisé(e)** braised
**grillé(e)** grilled

**Green**
for go ahead

**mariné(e)** marinated
**en purée** puréed, mashed

**au levain** leavened (with yeast)
**à la vapeur** steamed
**au vinaigre** with vinegar
**farci(e)** stuffed/filled
**frit(e)** fried
**fumé(e)** smoked
**rôti(e)** roasted/joint (meat)

**Amber**
for wait
and think

 29

Listen to the
green, amber and
red words being
pronounced and
repeat them,
visualising your
links and images
as you do.

### How to remember amber words:

| | |
|---|---|
| **au levain** | *Oh*! I have *eleven* rolls of bread! |
| **à la vapeur** | think of water *vapour*, which makes clouds of steam |
| **au vinaigre** | think of a *vinaigrette* salad dressing, which is made with vinegar |
| **farci** | imagine a *farce* where someone has the stuffing knocked out of them! |
| **frit** | the fried rice is *free* tonight! |
| **fumé** | think of *fumes*, a lot of smoke |
| **rôti** | imagine meeting the author of your favourite cookbook, the person who *wrote* 'E*asy* ways to roast meat' |

**au beurre** with butter
**à la broche** spit roasted
**à la coque** soft boiled (for eggs)
**grillé(e) au charbon de bois** chargrilled
**en papillotte** baked in foil
**au four** baked
**au plat** fried eggs (oeufs au plat)

**Red**
for stop, think,
make a link

### To help you memorise red words:

| | |
|---|---|
| **au beurre** | imagine picking the *burrs* your cat brought in out of the butter! |

| | |
|---|---|
| **à la broche** | imagine reading a *broch*ure about a new restaurant where they roast meat on a spit in front of the diners |
| **à la coque** | *cock*-a-doodle-doo! your soft boiled egg is ready! |
| **au charbon de bois** | *Oh! Char*lotte *Bon*ny likes char-grilled meat in the *Bois* de Boulogne (a famous park in Paris) |
| **au four** | imagine trying to fit a *four*-oven cooker in your kitchen! |
| **en papillotte** | what if you called your father *"Pappy"*? Would he like it a *lot*? |
| **au plat** | imagine finding fried eggs on the *plat*form at the train station |

## Activités de mémorisation
Memorising activities

**7. Match the names of the French dishes to their English equivalents:**

truite à la vapeur   pâtes au beurre   côtelettes de porc aux poivrons
poulet rôti   saumon en papillote   pommes de terre au four
œufs à la coque   sardines grillées   poulet à la broche

pork cutlets with peppers   pasta with butter   grilled sardines   soft-boiled eggs   steamed trout   spit-roasted chicken   roast chicken   oven-baked potatoes   foil-baked salmon

| French | English |
|---|---|
| 1. ................................ | 1. ................................ |
| 2. ................................ | 2. ................................ |

|   |   |   |   |
|---|---|---|---|
| 3. | ............... | 3. | ............... |
| 4. | ............... | 4. | ............... |
| 5. | ............... | 5. | ............... |
| 6. | ............... | 6. | ............... |
| 7. | ............... | 7. | ............... |
| 8. | ............... | 8. | ............... |
| 9. | ............... | 9. | ............... |

**8. Un bon repas. Complete the names of dishes using the words below:**

farcie   gratin   glace   courgettes   pois   gâteau   jambon

1. Entrée: Asperges au ............
2. Plat principal, légumes: ............... de ............... et de carottes
3. Plat principal: viande ou poisson: truite ............... aux petits ............
4. Dessert: ................. à la rhubarbe et ............. à la vanille

**9. Listen to the dialogues and complete the waiter's order forms:**

30

**Dialogue 1:**
Entrée: ...............................
Plat principal: ...............................
...............................
Dessert: ...............................

**Dialogue 2:**
Entrée: ...............................
Plat principal: ...............................
...............................
Dessert: ...............................

**Tony's Tip**

You'll learn food vocabulary best by practising while eating – so live it up a little! Go to your local French restaurant or prepare your own French dishes. Particularly if you are a tactile learner, it's the perfect opportunity to practise saying your new words while doing something physical – eating and drinking!

## Généralités  Basic information

To convey basic information about yourself, you will need the following structures:

Name: **je m'appelle** + (name and surname)   my name is …

Note the expressions:
**Mon prénom est John, mon nom de famille est Smith**
My name is John, my surname is Smith

Age: **j'ai** + (number) + **ans**   I am … years old

Residence: **j'habite à** + (town)/**j'habite en/au/aux** + (region, country)   I live in …

Nationality: **je suis** + (nationality)   I am …

Note the expression:
**je suis de** + (town)   I am from + (town)

Marital status: **je suis + célibataire/marié(e)/séparé(e)/divorcé(e)/veuf/veuve**   I am single/separated/divorced/a widower/a widow

**Green**
for go ahead

  31

Listen to the green words being pronounced and repeat them.

**Amber**
for wait and think

**anglais(e)** English
**américain(e)** American
**australien(ne)** Australian
**canadien(ne)** Canadian
**chinois(e)** Chinese
**divorcé(e)** divorced
**français(e)** French
**indien(ne)** Indian
**irlandais(e)** Irish

**italien(ne)** Italian
**japonais(e)** Japanese
**marié(e)** married
**néo-zélandais(e)** New Zealand
**nom** name
**nom de famille** surname
**pakistanais(e)** Pakistani
**résident(e)** resident
**séparé(e)** separated

**célibataire** single
**écossais(e)** Scottish
**espagnol(e)** Spanish
**étranger(ère)** foreign

**fils/fille** son/daughter
**gallois(e)** Welsh
**habiter** to live

### How to remember amber words:

**célibataire** — think of monks, they're *celibate*, they don't get married

**écossais(e)** — imagine being in a boat on a Scottish loch and hearing an *echo* – *say* it again!

**espagnol(e)** — think of a new type of *spaniel*, a Spanish one!

**étranger(ère)** — think of *eh! stranger!*

**fils/fille** — think of *filial*

**gallois(e)** — it's *gall*ing to be in England when you want to be in Wales!

**habiter** — think of a *habitat*, a place where people or animals live

**j'ai ...** I have ...
**je m'appelle ...** my name is ...
**près** near
**je suis ...** I am ...
**veuf/veuve** widower/widow

**Red**
for stop, think, make a link

32

Listen to the amber and red words being pronounced and repeat them, visualising your links and images as you do.

### To help you memorise red words:

**j'ai ...** — think of your best friend telling you, "I have a poster of *Che* Guevara on my wall"

**je m'appelle ...** — think of a red-cheeked lady saying "my name is *Ma Apple*"!

**près** — imagine a group of monks *pray*ing very close together

**je suis** — think of someone holding a cuckoo clock and saying "I am *Swiss*"!

**veuf/ve** — think of a Black Widow spider spinning its web very fast – with *verve*!

**Tony's Tip**

An easy and fun way to remember whether a French word is masculine or feminine, or whether an ending needs to be masculine or feminine, is to pick a super-masculine figure and associate every masculine word or ending with him. Then do the same with the feminine words and a super-feminine figure!

## Activités de mémorisation
Memorising activities

**1. Le drapeau. Write the corresponding nationality under each flag:**

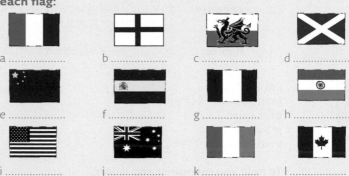

a ..................    b ..................    c ..................    d ..................

e ..................    f ..................    g ..................    h ..................

i ..................    j ..................    k ..................    l ..................

**2. Match the beginning of each word or expression with its correct ending:**

| Beginnings | Endings |
|---|---|
| 1. céli | a. nger |
| 2. rési | b. uf |
| 3. pr | c. bataire |
| 4. étra | d. dent |
| 5. fi | e. lois |
| 6. habi | f. ès de |
| 7. ve | g. lle |
| 8. gal | g. ter |

**3. Solve the anagrams of these words:**

1. CIVRODE
2. FUEV
3. EMIRA
4. RAESEP

**4. Add the missing letters to make four nationalities:**

1. __ d__ __ __ __ __
3. __ __ __ a __ __ a __ __

2. __ __ o__ __ __ __ s
4. __ __ __ l__ __ s

**5. Complete with four words or expressions used when talking about yourself:**

1. __ __  __ __ __ __ - __
3. __ __ __'__ __ __ __ __ __ __

2. __'__ __ __
4. __'__ __ __ __ __ __ __ __ __

**6. Complete the following introduction by John Smith, a 52-year-old divorced Glaswegian living in Manchester:**

Bonjour , ........................ John Smith, .................. Glasgow, mais
.................. Manchester. ...... 52 ......, et ...........................

## Au travail  Work

To convey basic information about your job or profession, you will need the following structures:

To say what your job/profession is:
**je suis** + (name of job/profession)   I am a ...

To say where you work:
**je travaille dans un/une** + (generic name of workplace)   I work in a ...

To say who or what kind of company you work for:
**je travaille pour** + (name of company)/**je travaille pour une** + (type of company)   I work for ...

To say what your job is like: **c'est un travail** + (adjective)   It's a ... job

**Green**
for go ahead

 33

Listen to the green words being pronounced and repeat them.

une agence publicitaire  advertising agency
une banque  bank
un bureau  office
un(e) chef  chef, cook
le/la dentiste  dentist
l'étudiant(e)  student
un hôpital  hospital
important(e)  important
intéressant(e)  interesting
le/la journaliste  journalist
un laboratoire  laboratory
le/la mécanicien(ne)  mechanic
une multinationale  a multinational
le/la pharmacien(ne)  pharmacist
un restaurant  restaurant
le/la secrétaire  secretary
stressant(e)  stressful

**Amber**
for wait
and think

 34

Listen to the amber and red words being pronounced and repeat them, visualising your links and images as you do.

agréable  pleasant
l'avocat(e)  solicitor
un cabinet d'avocats/médical  legal/medical practice
le/la commerçant(e)  shopkeeper
une compagnie d'assurance  insurance company
difficile  difficult
l'employé(e) de bureau  office worker
facile  easy
fatigant(e)  tiring
un homme/une femme au foyer  house husband/housewife
le magasin  shop
le médecin  doctor
le professeur  teacher
retraité(e)  retired
le serveur/la serveuse  waiter/waitress
le/la scientifique  scientist
travailler  to work

**How to remember amber words:**

agréable        what is *agreeable* is pleasant

assurance       similar to *assurance*: an insurance company gives you 'assurance'

| | |
|---|---|
| **avocat** | think of *advocate*, in the expression 'devil's advocate' |
| **cabinet** | imagine a practice full of *cabinets* to store all patients' data |
| **commerçant** | think of *commerce*, which also means trade |
| **employé(e)** | think of an office worker as an *employee* working at his/her desk |
| **facile** | think of *facile* and learn **facile** and **difficile** as a pair |
| **fatigant** | think of *fatigue*, another word for 'tired' |
| **homme/femme au foyer** | imagine a *femme* fatale standing in the *foyer* of a hotel who suddenly decides she wants to be a housewife after all! |
| **magasin** | think of a shop full of *magazines* |
| **médecin** | a doctor prescribes *medicine* |
| **professeur** | a *professor* teaches |
| **retraité** | think of a retired person who *retreated* to a quieter place to live |
| **scientifique** | think of *scientific* |
| **serveur/serveuse** | a waiter *serves* customers |
| **travailler** | think of someone who prefers to *travel*, yeah! instead of working |

**une école** school
**faire** to do/make
**ennuyeux(euse)** boring

**Red**
for stop, think,
make a link

**To help you memorise red words:**

| | |
|---|---|
| **école** | imagine a group of *eco*logists who have opened their own school |
| **faire** | think of the expression "*fair* do's!", or the fair trade slogan "Make trade *fair*" |
| **ennuyeux(euse)** | a boring, *annoying* job |

## Activités de mémorisation
Memorising activities

**7. Match the names of the French jobs to their English equivalents:**

médecin  avocat  mécanicien  professeur  pharmacien  journaliste
dentiste  chef  commerçant  serveur  étudiant  secrétaire

student  dentist  pharmacist  mechanic  solicitor  waiter  shopkeeper
doctor  secretary  teacher  chef  journalist

| Français | English |
|---|---|
| 1. ................................ | 1. ................................ |
| 2. ................................ | 2. ................................ |
| 3. ................................ | 3. ................................ |
| 4. ................................ | 4. ................................ |
| 5. ................................ | 5. ................................ |
| 6. ................................ | 6. ................................ |
| 7. ................................ | 7. ................................ |
| 8. ................................ | 8. ................................ |
| 9. ................................ | 9. ................................ |
| 10. ................................ | 10. ................................ |
| 11. ................................ | 11. ................................ |
| 12. ................................ | 12. ................................ |

**8. Le lieu de travail. Complete the names of workplaces using the endings below:**

-tionale   -que   -ce   -tal   -rant   -le   -toire   -asin   -inet   -eau

1. une agen–
2. un labora–
3. une multina–
4. un mag–
5. un restau–
6. un hôpi–
7. une éco–
8. un cab–
9. un bur–
10. une ban–

**9. Complete with the names of tour jobs:**

1. Je travaille dans un hôpital, je suis __ __ __ __ __ __ __. C'est un travail intéressant, mais c'est fatigant.

2. Je travaille dans une école, je suis __ __ __ __ __ __ __ __ __ __ __. C'est un travail stressant.

3. Je travaille dans un bar, je suis __ __ __ __ __ __ __. C'est un travail agréable.

4. Je travaille dans un bureau, je suis __ __ __ __ __ __ __ de __ __ __ __ __ __. C'est un travail un peu ennuyeux.

**10. Complete with the names of four workplaces:**

1. Je suis scientifique. Je travaille dans un __ __ __ __ __ __ __ __ __ __ __ __.

2. Je suis commerçant. Je travaille dans un __ __ __ __ __ __ __.

3. Je suis chef. Je travaille dans un __ __ __ __ __ __ __ __ __ __.

4. Je suis avocat. Je travaille pour un __ __ __ __ __ __ __ d' __ __ __ __ __ __ __.

35

**11. Listen to Anne and David talking about themselves and their jobs and complete the table:**

|  | Surname | Age | Job | Place of work | Job features |
|---|---|---|---|---|---|
| Anne |  |  |  |  |  |
| David |  |  |  |  |  |

# Allons un peu plus loin    Let's go a bit further

You can extend what you've learnt in this unit by adding some of the words and expressions you've learnt in Units 3 and 4.

**12. Read Charlotte Berger's profile, then complete the table below, with her details:**

Je m'appelle Charlotte Berger. Je mesure un mètre soixante-dix. J'ai quarante-six ans. Je suis née le trois août mille neuf cent soixante-trois. Je suis française, et je suis née à Bordeaux. En ce moment, j'habite au Canada, à Québec. J'habite 24 rue du château. Je suis divorcée et j'ai une fille. Je suis professeur. Je travaille dans un collège. Mon travail est stressant et fatigant, mais très intéressant. J'aime beaucoup travailler avec les adolescents.

Prénom:                          Adresse:
Nom:                             Etat civil:
Date de naissance:               Profession:
Lieu de naissance:               Age:
Nationalité:                     Taille:
Pays de résidence :

**13. Write a similar profile of yourself. If the job or workplace you need are not listed in this unit, look them up in a dictionary.**

## Pour finir: Mind Map it!

To exercise your memory, draw a Mind Map of the personal information you have learnt in this unit.

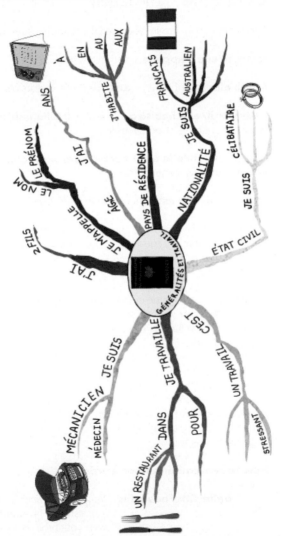

## La famille   The family

To talk about your family, you need the following structures:

Name: **il/elle s'appelle** + name   his/her name is …

Age: **il/elle a** + (number) + **ans**   she/he is … years old

Residence: **il/elle habite à** + (town) or **il/elle habite en/au/aux** + (region or country)   she/he lives in …

Marital status: **il/elle est + célibataire/séparé(e)/divorcé(e)/ veuf (veuve)**   she/he is single …

Profession: **il/elle est** + (name of job or profession)   she/he is a …

**Green**
for go ahead

le cousin  (male) cousin
la cousine  (female) cousin
maman  mum
la nièce  niece

l'oncle  uncle
papa  dad
les parents  parents

**Amber**
for wait
and think

 36

Listen to the green and amber words being pronounced and repeat them, visualising your links as you do.

la belle-fille  daughter-in-law / step-daughter
le beau-fils  son-in-law / step-son
l'enfant (f.) (m.)  child
la femme  wife
le fils  son
la fille  daughter
le mari  husband
le neveu  nephew
les petits-enfants  grandchildren
la petite-fille  granddaughter
le petit-fils  grandson

### How to remember amber words:

**belle-fille/beau-fils**   imagine tying *bows* in your in-laws' hair- your sister-in-law wants to charge a *fee*, while your brother-in-law thinks they should both charge *fees*

| | |
|---|---|
| **enfant** | think of an *infant*, a small child |
| **femme** | imagine a woman who is *fam*ished |
| **fils/fille** | think of your son charging higher *fees* than your daughter, her *fee* is much more reasonable! |
| **mari** | think of a woman complaining her husband has changed – "he's not the same man I *marri*ed!" |
| **neveu** | it sounds a bit like *nephew* |
| **petits-enfants** | grandchildren are *petite* when they are *infants* |
| **petit-fils/ petite-fille** | imagine a family in which all the grand-sons and grand-daughters are *petite* |

**le beau-frère** brother-in-law / step-brother
**le beau-père** father-in-law / step-father
**la belle-mère** mother-in-law/ step-mother
**la belle-soeur** sister-in-law / step-sister
**le frère** brother
**le gendre** son-in-law
**le grand-père** grandfather
**la grand-mère** grandmother
**la mère** mother
**le père** father
**la soeur** sister
**la tante** aunt

**Red**
for stop, think, make a link

(◎) 37

Listen to the red words being pronounced and repeat them, visualising your links and images as you do.

**To help you memorise red words:**

| | |
|---|---|
| **frère** | imagine a big family: first meet the oldest brother, he's always singing the *Frère* Jacques song |
| **beau-frère** | now meet the brother-in-law, who always wears a *bow* tie |

| | |
|---|---|
| **mère** | then there's the mother, who loves horses and owns a *mare* |
| **belle-mère** | the mother-in-law is keen on horses too, but she ties *bells* in her *mare*'s tail |
| **gendre** | as for the son-in-law, they're not sure what they'll call him when he changes his *gender* |
| **grand-père / grand-mère** | the *grand*father likes *pears*, but they give the *grand*mother night*mares* |
| **père** | luckily, the father can re*pair* anything |
| **beau-père** | the father-in-law is a bit eccentric – he ties a *bow* in his hair and likes climbing *pear* trees |
| **soeur** | the sister is a *surg*eon |
| **belle-soeur** | the sister-in-law wear *bells* to go *surf*ing |
| **tante** | the family have made up a chant for the aunt, which rhymes with *tante*, she's the assis*tant* of an impor*tant* accoun*tant* |

## Activités de mémorisation
Memorising activities

**1. Une famille nombreuse! Tidy up the words below, listing them with their articles in alphabetical order according to two categories: les hommes (men) and les femmes (women). If words indicate both, list them twice:**

belle-mère    fils    mari    tante    petit-fils    gendre    soeur
belle -soeur    neveu    cousine    femme    grand-mère    belle-fille
beau-père    papa    mère    cousin    oncle    grand-père
petite-fille    frère    père    nièce    maman    fille    beau-frère

## Les hommes

1. .............................
2. .............................
3. .............................
4. .............................
5. .............................
6. .............................
7. .............................
8. .............................
9. .............................
10. .............................
11. .............................
12. .............................
13. .............................

## Les femmes

1. .............................
2. .............................
3. .............................
4. .............................
5. .............................
6. .............................
7. .............................
8. .............................
9. .............................
10. .............................
11. .............................
12. .............................
13. .............................

**2. Solve the anagrams to find members of the family:**

1. TAFENN
2. NETTA
3. REGNED
4. LOREBLUSEE

**3. Add the missing letters to make the names of four relatives beginning with F:**

1. __ e__ __ __
2. __ __ e__ __ __

3. __ i__ __ __
4. __ __ __l__ __ __

**4. L'arbre généalogique: look at Julien's family tree, imagine you are Julien and complete the following sentences:**

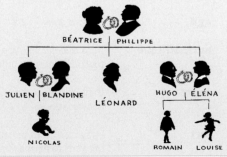

BÉATRICE | PHILIPPE

JULIEN | BLANDINE
LÉONARD
HUGO | ÉLÉNA

NICOLAS

ROMAIN   LOUISE

1. Philippe est mon .........., Béatrice est ma ..........
2. Blandine est ma .........., Léonard est mon ............
3. Éléna est ma ......., Hugo est mon ..............
4. Nicolas est mon ..........., Romain est mon ..............

## Les gens  People

To describe people, you need the following structures:

Hair: **il/elle a les cheveux** + colour/length/appearance  she/he has ... hair

Eyes: **il/elle a les yeux** + colour  she/he has ... eyes

Physical appearance/personality: **il/elle est** + adjective  she/he is ...

**Green**
for go ahead

 38

Listen to the green words being pronounced and repeat them.

**amusant(e)** amusing
**blond(e)** blond
**curieux(se)** curious
**extraverti(e)** extrovert
**généreux(se)** generous
**jaloux(se)** jealous
**impatient(e)** impatient
**intelligent(e)** intelligent

**intéressant(e)** interesting
**introverti(e)** introverted
**long(ue)** long (e.g. of hair)
**nerveux(euse)** nervous
**patient(e)** patient
**sérieux(euse)** serious, dependable
**timide** shy

**agé(e)** elderly
**antipathique** unpleasant, not friendly
**court(e)** short (e.g. in length)
**fort(e)** stout, chubby
**frisé(e)(s)** curly (of hair)
**grand(e)** tall

**joli(e)** pretty
**maigre** thin
**marron** brown (eyes)
**petit(e)** short, small (e.g. in height)
**séduisant(e)** attractive
**sympathique** friendly, pleasant

**Amber**
for wait and think

 39

Listen to the amber and red words being pronounced and repeat them, visualising your links and images as you do.

### How to remember amber words:

| | |
|---|---|
| **agé** | think of *aged* |
| **antipathique** | think of *antipathy*, you might feel *antipathy* towards someone unfriendly and unpleasant |
| **court** | think of *curt*: curt remarks make short conversations! |
| **fort** | imagine a stout person who makes a lot of *effort*s to earn a *fort*une playing the piano*forte* |

| | |
|---|---|
| **frisé** | it sounds very similar to *frizzy* |
| **grand** | think of a *grand* piano |
| **joli** | imagine a *jolly* pretty girl |
| **maigre** | think of *meagre* |
| **marron** | think of marrons glacés – crystallised chestnuts – delicious! |
| **petit** | think of the "*petite*" section in clothes shops, for women who are shorter than average |
| **séduisant** | think of *seduced* – when someone is attractive, you may be seduced by him or her |
| **sympatique** | is similar to *sympathetic:* if someone is *sympathetic*, they are likely to be nice (it's the opposite to **antipathique**, which you saw earlier) |

**Red**
for stop, think,
make a link

**châtain(s)** brown (of hair), chestnut-haired
**les cheveux (m.)** hair
**ennuyeux(euse)** boring
**jeune** young
**laid(e)** ugly
**mignon(ne)** pretty

**mince** slim
**ondulé(e)(s)** wavy (of hair)
**raide(s)** straight (of hair)
**roux(sse)** red (of hair)
**les yeux** eyes

**To help you memorise red words:**

| | |
|---|---|
| **châtains** | imagine having a *chat* with a pair of chestnut-haired submarine cap*tains*! |
| **cheveux** | imagine a di*shevelled* man, with wild untidy hair |
| **ennuyeux** | think of *annoying* and imagine a boring person droning on and on at a party … |

| | |
|---|---|
| **jeune** | imagine a meeting that has to ad*journ* because the room has been invaded by young children! |
| **laid** | imagine a horribly ugly *lead* statue disp*layed* in an exhibition |
| **mignon** | imagine a pretty *minion* |
| **mince** | imagine a thin man eating a plate of lean, finely *minced* beef |
| **ondulé** | think of *undulate* – *undulating* roads look like waves |
| **raide** | it sounds like 'red'. Imagine a girl with straight red hair, dressed in a straight red dress. |
| **roux** | imagine a ginger kanga*roo* bouncing around your living room! |
| **yeux** | it sounds like "yer"! imagine someone saying "Are *yer* tired? *Yer* eyes are pink!" |

## Activités de mémorisation
Memorising activities

**5. Put the adjectives below in pairs of opposites, according to their meaning and ending:**

antipathique  ennuyeux  jeune  frisés  joli  laid  maigre  amusant
raides  fort  vieux  sympathique

| | | | |
|---|---|---|---|
| 1. .................... | | 1. .................... | |
| 2. .................... | | 2. .................... | |
| 3. .................... | **VS** | 3. .................... | |
| 4. .................... | | 4. .................... | |
| 5. .................... | | 5. .................... | |
| 6. .................... | | 6. .................... | |

**6. Complete the words using one of the beginnings below:**

ner–  jo–  mig–  fri–  tim–  cur–  géné–  min–  ja–  sér

1. –sés
2. –ce
3. –non
4. –li

5. –ieux
6. –ide
7. –veux
8. –reux

9. –ieux
10. –loux

**7. Il/elle a les cheveux ... Add the missing letters to make four adjectives which describe hair:**

1. b _ _ _ _ s

3. f_ _ _ _ _ _

2. _ _ i _ _ _ _

4. _ _ d_ _ _ _ _

**8. Il/elle est comment? Add the missing letters to make four words which describe physical appearance:**

1. _ _ r _ _

3. _ _ _ g _ _ _

2. _ _ n _ _ _

4. _ _ a _ _ _

**9. Listen to the descriptions and say who is being described:**

40

go to
www.collinslanguage.com/revolution
for extra activities

soixante-quinze  75

## Parler du temps Talking about the weather

To describe the weather, you need the following structure:
**Il.../il est.../il fait.../il y a ...** + type of weather   It's ... + weather
**Le temps est ...** + type of weather   The weather is ...

Sometimes the weather word stays the same (**la neige**, **il neige**, snow, it's snowing), sometimes it changes (**la pluie**, **il pleut**, rain, it's raining).

**Green**
for go ahead

 41

Listen to the green words being pronounced and repeat them, thinking of their meaning as you do.

l'automne (f.)  autumn
le climat  climate
l'est (m.)  East
les degrés (m.)  degrees (centigrade), °C
humide  humid, damp
l'humidité (f.)  humidity, dampness

le nord  North
l'ouest (m.)  West
le sud  South
la température  temperature
zéro  zero

**beau/il fait beau**  good/the weather is good
**la brume/le temps est brumeux**  mist/it's misty
**chaud/il fait chaud**  hot/it's warm, hot
**l'éclaircie (f.)**  clear/sunny spell
**frais/il fait frais**  chilly (or fresh)/it's chilly
**froid/il fait froid**  cold/it's cold
**la météo**  weather forecast
**le soleil/il fait soleil**  sun/it's sunny
**la tempête**  storm (wind or sea)
**le vent/il y a du vent/il fait du vent**  wind/it's windy

**Amber**
for wait and think

 42

Listen to the amber and red words being pronounced and repeat them, visualising your links and images as you do.

### How to remember amber words:

| | |
|---|---|
| **beau** | when the weather is good, girls tie *bow*s in their hair |
| **brume** | think of trying to sweep away the mist with a *broom* |
| **brumeux** | if you're sweeping the mist away with a *broom*, does that make you a *broomer*? |
| **chaud** | imagine an outdoor *show* in August, when the weather is really hot! |

| éclaircie | When there is a sunny spell the sky is *clear* – think of eating *éclairs* under a clear blue sky |
|---|---|
| **frais** | think of fresh, sometimes we say the weather is 'a bit fresh', or remember the *fray*ed edges around the frost in your freezer – time to defrost it! |
| **froid** | we use the expression *sang froid* in English, meaning cold blood |
| **météo** | think of *mete*orology |
| **soleil** | think of *solar* energy |
| **tempête** | think of *tempest*, which is a violent storm |
| **vent** | think of *vent*ilator |

**Red**
for stop, think,
make a link

**le brouillard/il y a du brouillard**  fog/it's foggy
**la chaleur**  heat
**le ciel**  sky
**l'été (m.)**  summer
**étouffant**  muggy
**la gelée /il gèle**  frost, it's freezing
**la grêle/il grêle**  hail/it's hailing
**l'hiver (m.)**  winter
**mauvais/il fait mauvais**  bad/the weather is bad
**la neige/il neige**  snow/it's snowing
**le nuage/il fait nuageux**  cloud/it's cloudy
**l'orage (m.)**  thunderstorm
**la pluie**  rain
**il pleut**  it's raining
**le printemps**  spring
**le verglas/verglacé(e)**  black ice/icy (of roads)

**To help you memorise red words:**

| brouillard | imagine trying to *brew* some tea in the *yard* on a foggy day |
|---|---|
| chaleur | think how nice it is to come back to a warm *chalet* after skiing |

| | |
|---|---|
| **ciel** | did you *see ele*phants in the sky last night? |
| **été** | in the summer, it's nice to eat outside at a *ta*ble on a *te*rrace |
| **étouffant** | *Eh*! the weather is *too* hot! I need a *fan*! |
| **gelée** | imagine someone wearing frosty-looking hair*gel* at a party |
| **grêle** | the sky is *grey* when it *hails* |
| **hiver** | in the winter, you often catch a *fever* |
| **mauvais** | bad weather is not the time to *mow* your lawn, however *vai*n you are about it! |
| **neige** | imagine teen*ager*s who ma*nage* to snowboard in a snowstorm |
| **nuage** | imagine a bunch of '*new-ager*s' camping on a cloudy weekend |
| **nuageux** | imagine a *new-ager* living in the cloudy region at the top of a mountain |
| **orage** | *Oh! Rage!* a thunderstorm! |
| **pluie** | pluie sounds a bit like *plea*, so you could *plea*d for it not to rain on your birthday |
| **pleut** | think of rain always being *plur*al – so when it's raining, you never get a single drop on its own |
| **printemps** | think of *spring time* |
| **verglas** | black ice is *very glass*y |
| **verglacé** | think of a car skidding on frozen *glacé* cherries |

## Activités de mémorisation
Memorising activities

**1. Quel temps fait-il? Say what the weather is like by matching each picture with the correct expression:**

a .................................    b .................................    c .................................

d .................................    e .................................    f .................................

g .................................    h .................................

1. Il fait froid.
2. Il fait nuageux.
3. Il fait chaud.
4. Il fait beau, il y a du soleil.

5. Il pleut.
6. Il y a du vent.
7. Il neige.
8. Il y a du brouillard.

**2. Complete the words using one of the endings below:**

−pête    −lée    −age    −rcie    −age    −ie    −ge

1. éclai−
2. plu−
3. nu−
4. or−

5.      nei−
6.      ge−
7.      tem−

**3. Solve the anagrams of these words related to the weather:**

1. MITALC
2. VALGRES

3. REHUCLA
4. RIFAS

**4. Add the missing letters to make four words to complete the expression: il ...**

1. __ e __ __ __

3. __ __ __ g __

2. __ __ __ __ u __

4. __ __ __ __l __

**5. Complete with four expressions which can follow "il fait":**

1. __ e __ __ __

3. __ __ __ __ u __

2. __ __ __ o __ __ __

4. __ __ __ u __ __ __ __

**6. Le temps en France: look at the map and complete the following sentences:**

1. Dans le nord, il ...
2. Dans l'ouest, il ... et ...
3. Dans l'est, ...
4. Dans le sud, ...

# Les prévisions météorologiques/la météo The weather forecast

**Green**
for go ahead

 43

Listen to the green and amber words being pronounced and repeat them, visualising your links as you do.

**automnal(e)** autumnal
**central(e)** central
**de l'est** eastern, from the East
**instable** unstable, changing
**intense** intense
**local(e)** local
**maximal(e)** maximum (of temperature)
**minimal(e)** minimum (of temperature)
**du nord** northern, from the North
**de l'ouest** western, from the West
**les précipitations (f.)** precipitation, rain
**la pression** pressure
**la région** region
**stable** stable
**du sud** southern, from the South
**variable** variable, changing

**Amber**
for wait and think

**agité(e)** rough (of the sea), choppy
**amélioration (f.)** improving
**en baisse** decreasing
**basse pression** low pressure
**détérioration (f.)** getting worse
**en hausse** increasing
**haute pression** high pressure
**la mer** sea
**nocturne** night-time

## How to remember amber words:

| | |
|---|---|
| **agité** | think of *agitated* |
| **amélioration** | think of *amelioration* (improvement) |
| **en baisse** | *Bess!* Take your coat, the temperature is dropping! |
| **basse** | think of the double-*bass*, a low-pitched instrument |
| **détérioration** | think of *deteriorate* |

| | |
|---|---|
| **hausse** | temperatures go up when the pressure increases – that's when you need to get your *hose* out and water the grass |
| **haute** | think of *haute* couture, high fashion at very high prices! |
| **mer** | think of having a *merry* time by the sea |
| **nocturne** | think of *nocturnal* |

**l'averse (f.)**  shower (rain)
**dégagé(e)**  clear (of sky)
**doux/douce**  mild
**estival(e)**  summery
**fort(e)**  rough (of sea)
**glacial(e)**  icy
**hivernal(e)**  wintery
**lourd(e)**  sultry, heavy (like before a storm)
**printanier(ère)**  spring-like
**au-dessus de zéro**  above zero
**en dessous de zéro**  below freezing, sub-zero

**Red**
for stop, think, make a link

44

Listen to the red words being pronounced and repeat them, visualising your images as you do.

**To help you memorise red words:**

| | |
|---|---|
| **averse** | I am *averse* to showers during my barbecue |
| **dégagé** | think of *disengaged*: when the sky is clear, the clouds have disengaged! |
| **doux** | imagine Scooby-*doo* having to put away his toboggan when the weather gets mild and the snow melts |
| **estival** | it's easy to be *festive* if the weather is summery |
| **glacial** | think of *glacier* |
| **hivernal** | if you think of two bears called Vernon and Al hibernating in the winter, then you'll remember to swap the 'b' in *hibern*ate for a 'v' and put *al* on the end! |

| | |
|---|---|
| **lourd** | imagine a *Lord* doing weightlifting |
| **printanier** | in the *spring Tania* likes to wear green colours |
| **au-dessus** | imagine Shakespeare sitting in the sunshine writing an *ode* for *Sue* |
| **en dessous** | imagine the *Andes* climbed by *Sue* in freezing weather |

## Activités de mémorisation
### Memorising activities

**7. Divide the expressions below into two categories: beau temps (nice weather) and mauvais temps (bad weather):**

le ciel est dégagé – tout est verglacé – les températures sont stables – la température maximale est de 25°C – la température minimale est de 18° C – il gèle – le ciel est nuageux – la température maximale est de 5°C

**beau temps**

1. ...............................
2. ...............................
3. ...............................
4. ...............................
5 ...............................

**mauvais temps**

a. ...............................
b. ...............................
c. ...............................
d. ...............................
e. ...............................

**8. Add the missing letters to make three words to describe the weather in January:**

1. _ _ _ O _ _ _

2. _ _ _ V _ _ _ _ _ _

3. _ _ L _ _ _ _ _ _

**9. Listen to the weather forecast and fill in the missing words:**

**45**

**Forecast 1**

................ du temps dans toute la France: localement ........... avec des ........... le matin, particulièrement dans le centre et l'......... Des averses

plus .......... dans .........., et des orages dans l'après-midi dans le ........
et le .................... ................ dans les autres régions. Températures
en ................ Vent d'ouest et mer ...................... à agitée, avec des
................ locales.

**Forecast 2**

Beau temps avec du .................. dans le sud et le sud-ouest, avec des
températures ................ et .................. Soleil également dans le nord
et l'est le matin, avec des ............. et des ...................... localement, et
de la .................. sur les Alpes. Dans les autres régions, ciel ................ et
....................

# Allons un peu plus loin
## Let's go a bit further

**12. Find the French for the following expressions in the box below:**

1. Clear skies with maybe a few clouds
2. Foggy patches
3. Occasionally intense rain and possible thunderstorms
4. Persistent rain all over France
5. Night-time temperature below freezing

nappes de brouillard    fortes pluies à caractère orageux
ciel dégagé avec quelques passages nuageux    pluies persistantes sur
tout le pays    minimales nocturnes en dessous de zéro

**Tony's Tip**

**The vocabulary tin**
To test your vocabulary, write the words you want to memorise over a week
on pieces of paper or card, French on one side and English on the other.
Then put them in a tin. Every day, pick five or ten words out of the tin. If
you read the English side first, try to remember the French, and vice versa.

If you get the word right, leave it out. If you don't, write the same word on
another piece of paper and put both back in the tin, to double your chance
of picking it out again.

## Pour finir: Mind Map it!

To exercise your memory, draw a mind map of the weather-related expressions you've learnt in this unit.

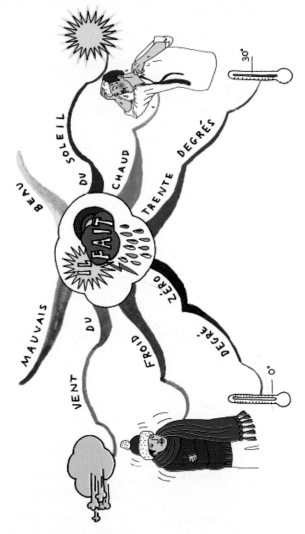

## La santé  Health

**Green**
for go ahead

 46

Listen to the grèen words being pronounced and repeat them, thinking of their meaning as you do.

l'allergie (f.)  allergy
allergique  allergic
l'antihistaminique (m.)  anti-histamine
l'aspirine (f.)  aspirin
les antibiotiques (m.)  antibiotics
le décongestionnant  decongestant
une indigestion  indigestion
une infection  infection
la nausée  nausea, feeling sick
le paracétamol  paracetamol
la pastille  pastille, lozenge
la pharmacie  chemist's, pharmacy
le sirop  cough syrup
le thermomètre  thermometer

**Amber**
for wait
and think

 47

Listen to the amber and red words being pronounced and repeat them, visualising your links and images as you do.

je vais bien  I'm well
je vais mal  I'm unwell, poorly
la fièvre  fever, (body) temperature
le médicament  medicine
la tension  (blood) pressure

### How to remember amber words:

| | |
|---|---|
| **bien** | think of an am*bien*ce that makes you feel good |
| **mal** | think of *mal*evolent and *mal*practice–both are bad |
| **fièvre** | think of *fever*ish |
| **médicament** | when you have a health predicament, you need a *medicament*! |
| **tension** | think of *tension* and how *tense* you might feel if you have high blood pressure |

**Red**
for stop, think,
make a link

**un comprimé (pour)** tablet (for)
**une grippe** flu
**un rhume** cold (ailment)
**je tousse** I have a cough
**une toux** cough

**How to remember red words:**

| | |
|---|---|
| **comprimé** | insist you won't *comprom*ise your health. You must have the tablets! |
| **grippe** | it's difficult to keep a *grip* on yourself when you have the flu |
| **rhume** | imagine being in the doctor's waiting *room* and everyone around you is coughing and sneezing |
| **tousse** | imagine you've got *two* sandwiches for lunch but you can't eat them because you've got a cough! |
| **toux** | one cough, *two* coughs, you should definitely stay in bed! |

## Activités de mémorisation
Memorising activities

**1. Divide the words below into two categories, maladies (ailments) and remèdes (remedies):**

médicament   fièvre   toux   pastille   sirop   rhume   grippe
antibiotique   tension   comprimé

**Maladies**

1. ...............................
2. ...............................
3. ...............................
4. ...............................
5. ...............................

**Remèdes**

1. ...............................
2. ...............................
3. ...............................
4. ...............................
5. ...............................

**2. Match each ailment to its correct remedy:**

1. une infection
2. de la fièvre
3. la toux
4. l'allergie
5. un rhume
6. la nausée

a. antihistaminique
b. médicament contre la nausée
c. antibiotique
d. décongestionnant
e. sirop
f. paracétamol

**3. Solve the anagrams of these ailments:**

1. PERGIP
2. SEITONGIDIN

3. VEFERI
4. SEUNAE

**4. Add the missing letters to make four remedies:**

1. ___ s ___ ___ ___ ___ ___ ___

2. ___ ___ t ___ ___ ___ ___ ___ ___ ___ ___ ___

3. ___ ___ ___ t ___ ___ ___ ___

4. ___ i ___ ___ ___

**5. Complete with four ailments that can follow "j'ai":**

1. ___ ___ ___ h ___ ___ ___ ___

2. ___ ___ ___ ___ ___ s ___ ___

3. ___ ___ ___ ___ i ___ ___ ___

4. ___ ___ ___ ___ ___ ___ ___ ___ e

**6. Je ne vais pas bien, j'ai …. Write under the pictures what the problem is:**

a. J'ai ……………    b. J'ai ……………    c. J'ai ……………

## Les parties du corps  Parts of the body

l'estomac (m.)  stomach, tummy

**le bras**  arm
**la dent, les dents**  tooth, teeth
**l'épaule (f.)**  shoulder
**le(s) genou(x)**  knee (knees)
**la gorge**  throat
**le pied**  foot
**la tête**  head

### How to remember amber words:

| | |
|---|---|
| **bras** | think of shouting *bra*vo! at the theatre and clapping with your arms in the air |
| **dent** | think of *dent*ist |
| **épaule** | think of *épaule*ttes |
| **genou** | think of *genuflect*, which means to bend one's knees |
| **gorge** | it makes your *gorge* rise to have a sore throat |
| **pied** | think of *pede*strian, someone travelling on foot, and *pied-à-terre* |
| **tête** | think of a *tête-à-tête* conversation |

**la cheville**  ankle
**le cou**  neck
**le coude**  elbow
**le(s) doigt(s)**  finger (fingers)
**le dos**  back
**la jambe**  leg
**la joue**  cheek
**la main**  hand
**l'oeil (les yeux) (m.)**  eye(s)
**l'oreille (f.)**  ear
**le poignet**  wrist

**Green**
for go ahead

48

Listen to the green and amber words being pronounced and repeat them, visualising your links as you do.

**Amber**
for wait
and think

**Red**
for stop, think, make a link

49

Listen to the red words being pronounced and repeat them, visualising your images as you do.

**la poitrine** chest
**le ventre** belly

## How to remember red words:

| | |
|---|---|
| **cheville** | imagine being di*shevelle*d because you broke your ankle |
| **cou** | doing too many sudo*ku*s can make your neck sore! |
| **coude** | imagine someone who *cooed* and flapped their elbows to imitate a bird |
| **doigt** | make an 'o' with your *digits* – now you know which letter to swap for the first 'i' in digit and you're almost there |
| **dos** | think of Homer Simpson with a backache... "*Doh*!" |
| **jambe** | think of dropping your sandwich and getting *jam* on your legs |
| **joue** | imagine *Ju*dy in a Punch and *Ju*dy puppet show – she has big red cheeks |
| **main** | think of *man*ufacture, making something with your hands |
| **oeil** | *Oy!* What happened to your eye? |
| **oreille** | *Oh! Ray! Yer* ears are so small! |
| **poignet** | imagine a *poignant* scene where a tennis player hurts his wrist in the final at Wimbledon |
| **poitrine** | don't try to run a marathon when your chest hurts! *Pottering* around is better |
| **ventre** | think of a *ventri*loquist, whose voice seems to come from his/her stomach |

## Activités de mémorisation
Memorising activities

**7. Match each French word in the first set with its English equivalent in the second set:**

dos  ventre  poitrine  oeil  oreille  dent  joue  doigt  poignet  gorge

cheek  wrist  chest  belly  finger  ear  eye  throat  back  tooth

| French | English |
|---|---|
| 1. .............................. | 1. .............................. |
| 2. .............................. | 2. .............................. |
| 3. .............................. | 3. .............................. |
| 4. .............................. | 4. .............................. |
| 5. .............................. | 5. .............................. |
| 6. .............................. | 6. .............................. |
| 7. .............................. | 7. .............................. |
| 8. .............................. | 8. .............................. |
| 9. .............................. | 9. .............................. |
| 10. .............................. | 10. .............................. |

**8. Complete the words using one of the beginnings below:**

do–   poi–   tê–   poi–   cou–   che–   ma–

1.  –te             4.  –igt              7.  –gnet
2.  –ville          5.  –in
3.  –trine          6.  –de

**9. Add the missing letters to make four words for parts of the upper body:**

1.  c __ __          3.  __ __ __ __ l __
2.  p __ __ __ __ __ __ __   4.  __ __ a __

**Tony's Tip**

**Labelling pictures**
To practise words for parts of the body, cut out pictures of a few celebrities or models from a glossy magazine. Write the French words for the parts of the body on Post-it labels, then see if you can stick them on the correct parts of the pictures. Say the words aloud as you do it. Associating the image and the sound will help you to remember the words.

**10. Add the missing letters to make four words for parts of the lower body:**

1. __ __ n __ __ e

3. __ __ m __ __ __

2. __ __ __ o __

4. __ i __ __ __

**11. Label the parts of the body:**

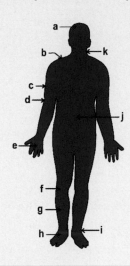

## Allons un peu plus loin
Let's go a bit further

To talk about your health, you need the following structures:

**j'ai** + name of ailment or illness

**j'ai de la fièvre/un rhume/la nausée/la grippe/une infection/ une allergie**
I have a temperature/a cold/I feel sick/I have flu/an infection/an allergy

**j'ai mal au/à la/à l'/aux** + part of the body that aches, hurts or is sore

**j'ai mal à l'estomac/aux dents/au dos/à la tête/au ventre/
aux oreilles/à la gorge/au pied**
I have stomach/tooth/back/a head/belly/ear ache/a sore throat /
my foot hurts

**je suis allergique au lait /à la poussière/au pollen**
I am allergic to milk/dust/pollen

## Activités de mémorisation
### Memorising activities

**12. Aches and pains: how would Louis say that the body parts
labelled ache or hurt?**

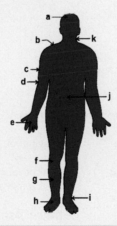

**13. Listen to the conversation between the pharmacist and a
customer and complete the following information in English:**

**Ailments:**

**Suggested remedies:**

**go to
www.collinslanguage.com/revolution
for extra activities**

## Le sport Sport

**Green**
for go ahead

 51

Listen to the green words being pronounced and repeat them, thinking of their meaning as you do.

l'aérobic (m.)  aerobics
l'athlétisme (m.)  athletics
le badminton  badminton
le basket(ball)  basketball
le cyclisme  cycling
le foot(ball)  football
la gymnastique  gymnastics
le golf  golf
le rugby  rugby
le ski  skiing
le squash  squash
le surf  surf
le tennis  tennis
le volley(ball)  volleyball
le yoga  yoga

**Amber**
for wait and think

 52

Listen to the amber and red words being pronounced and repeat them, visualising your links and images as you do.

l'alpinisme (m.)  mountaineering
le foot à cinq  five-a-side football
le footing  jogging

### How to remember amber words:

| | |
|---|---|
| **alpinisme** | imagine you are mountaineering in the *Alps* |
| **foot à cinq** | think of your *foot sink*ing in a puddle while playing five-a-side football |
| **footing** | think of jogging as putting your fitness on a sound *footing* |

**Red**
for stop, think, make a link

l'aviron (m.)  rowing
l'équitation (f.)  horse riding
l'escalade (f.)  rock climbing
la natation  swimming
la plongée  scuba diving
la randonnée  trekking, trek
le vélo  cycling, bike

**To help you memorise red words:**

| | |
|---|---|
| **aviron** | c'est *la vie Ron*, let's go rowing! |
| **équitation** | think of *equitation*, another word for horse riding |
| **escalade** | imagine how easy it would be to climb Mount Everest if there were *escalat*ors all the way up! |
| **natation** | imagine trying to make some *notations* while swimming! |
| **plongée** | imagine you are *plunging* into the sea to go scuba diving |
| **randonnée** | let's pick our next trek at *random, eh?* |
| **vélo** | think of a *velo*ciraptor on a bike, chasing you! |

To talk about which sport you do or play, you need the following structures:

**je fais du/de la/ de l'/ des** + name of sport

**je fais de l'aérobic/ de l'athlétisme /de la gymnastique/ du yoga/ du cyclisme /du footing/ du ski/de la natation/ de l'équitation**
I do aerobics/athletics/gymnastics/yoga/I cycle/I jog/I ski/I swim/I go horse riding

**je joue au** + name of team or racquet/club sport

**je joue au golf/ rugby/ tennis/ badminton / squash/ foot/ foot à cinq/ basket / volley**
I play golf/rugby/tennis/badminton/squash/football/five-a-side/basketball/volleyball

## Activités de mémorisation
Memorising activities

**1. Divide the words below into two categories: sport individuel (individual sports) and sport d'équipe (team sports):**

foot   yoga   golf   badminton   tennis   athlétisme   équitation
basket   aviron   foot à cinq   cyclisme

**Sport individuel**

1. .................................
2. .................................
3. .................................
4. .................................
5. .................................
6. .................................
7. .................................
8. .................................

**Sport d'équipe**

1. .................................
2. .................................
3. .................................
4. .................................
5. .................................
6. .................................

**2. Match each beginning with its correct ending to make the names of sports:**

1. l'équi
2. le vé
3. la nat
4. la plon
5. l'avi
6. l'athl
7. l'esca
8. le foo

a. gée
b. tation
c. lade
d. lo
e. ting
f. ation
g. ron
h. étisme

**3. Solve the anagrams of these names of sports:**

1. TEMISALETH
2. DALACESE

3. RINOVA
4. ATITUQINEO

**4. Add the missing letters to make four names of sports:**

1. __ e __ __ __ __ __

3. __ __ __ __ o __ __ __ __

2. __ __ __ o __

4. __ __ t __ __ __ __ __ __

**5. Je joue à... Write under the pictures what sport is being played:**

a                    b                    c                    d                    e

a. Je joue au .............  b. Je joue au .............  c. Je joue au .............

d. Je joue au .............  e. Je joue au .............

**6. Je fais... Write under the pictures what sport is being played:**

a                    b                    c                    d

a. Je fais ...................  b. Je fais ...................  c. Je fais ...................

d. Je fais ...................

## **Les loisirs** Leisure activities

**Green**
for go ahead

 53

Listen to the green and amber words being pronounced and repeat them, visualising your links as you do.

**aller au cinéma** to go to the cinema
**aller en boîte (de nuit)** to go to a disco
**aller à la gym** to go to the gym
**aller à la montagne** to go to the mountains
**aller au restaurant** to go to a restaurant
**aller au théâtre** to go to the theatre
**faire du shopping** to go shopping
**surfer sur internet** to surf the internet
**visiter un musée** to visit a museum

**Amber**
for wait
and think

**regarder la télé**  to watch TV
**rester à la maison**  to stay at home
**se faire bronzer**  to sunbathe

**How to remember amber words:**

| | |
|---|---|
| **regarder** | link it with *guard* – a guard watches CCTV screens |
| **maison** | think of a house built by a stone*mason* |
| **rester** | you can *rest* when you stay at home |
| **se faire bronzer** | people sunbathing hope they'll turn a nice *bronz*e colour |

**Red**
for stop, think,
make a link

 54

Listen to the red
words being
pronounced and
repeat them,
visualising your
images as you do.

**aller à la piscine**  to go to the swimming-pool
**aller à la plage**  to go to the beach
**écouter de la musique**  to listen to music
**jardiner**  to do gardening
**jouer aux cartes**  to play cards
**jouer du piano/de la guitare**  to play the piano/the guitar
**lire**  to read
**manger chez des amis**  to eat out at friends'
**sortir avec des amis**  to go out with friends
**sortir prendre un verre**  to go for a drink

**To help you memorise red words:**

| | |
|---|---|
| **piscine** | imagine yourself on holiday and trying to get some *peace* in the swimming-pool, floating on a comfortable airbed |
| **plage** | imagine a beach in the middle of a *plaza* |
| **écouter** | imagine the *accoutre*ments you need to listen to music: headphones, mp3 player, etc. |
| **jardiner** | imagine you like filling *jardinières* in your garden with plants |

| | |
|---|---|
| **jouer** | imagine a little girl who likes to play with *jewe*ls |
| **lire** | many British teenagers must read King *Lear* at school |
| **manger** | think of a horse eating from a *manger* in a stable |
| **sortir** | imagine someone who spends hours *sorting* out what they're wearing before they go out |
| **verre** | imagine going for a drink with a friend called *Ve*ra |

*Tony's Tip*

**The twin pillars of language learning**
Imagination and association are the twin pillars of your language learning. To help you remember new words, always link them to memorable images and **associate** them with something you already know. The more vividly you can **imagine** the pictures that represent the words you are learning, the faster you'll learn the new language.

## Activités de mémorisation
Memorising activities

**7. Match each French word or expression below with the correct picture:**

aller faire du shopping   sortir avec des amis   aller en boîte   jouer aux cartes   lire   regarder la télé   surfer sur Internet   aller à la plage   aller à la piscine

a .................. 　　　　b .................. 　　　　c ..................

d .................... e .................... f ....................

g .................... h .................... i ....................

**8. Complete the expressions using the endings below:**

-néma  -urant  -scine  -ison  -éâtre  -iner  -tagne  -rre  -ano

1. jard-
2. aller au ci-
3. aller au th-
4. aller à la mon-
5. aller au resta-

6. rester à la ma-
7. aller à la pi-
8. sortir prendre un ve-
9. jouer du pi-

**9. Rester a la maison ou sortir? Add the missing letters for two leisure activities you do at home and two you do outdoors.**

1. __ __ g __ __ __ __ __   __ __ __   __ __ __ __ __

2. __ __ __ f __ __ __   __ __ __ __   __ ' __ __ __ __ __ __ __ __ __ __

3. __ __ r __ __ __ __ __

4. __ __ l __ __ __ __ __ __ __ __ __ g __

 55

**10. Fill in the missing expressions, then listen to check:**

- Qu'est-ce que tu as comme loisirs?
- D'habitude, j'aime (to go for a drink) ou bien (to go out with friends).
  A la maison, j'aime (to listen to music) ou bien (to surf the Internet).
  Et toi?
- Moi, j'aime (to read) et (to do gardening).

## Allons un peu plus loin
Let's go a bit further

To express likes, dislikes and preferences, you need the following structures:

**j'aime (beaucoup)** + the name of the activity you like very much

**j'aime (beaucoup) le golf/lire/aller faire du shopping**
I like golf/reading/going shopping (very much)

**je n'aime pas (du tout)** + the name of the activity you don't like (at all)

**je n'aime pas (du tout) le foot/regarder la télé**
I don't like football/watching TV (at all)

**je voudrais/j'aimerais** + the name of the activity you would like to do

**je voudrais/j'aimerais aller au cinéma/jouer au volley**
I would like to go to the cinema/to play volleyball

**je n'ai pas envie de** + the name of the activity you (don't) feel like doing

**je n'ai pas envie de/d'aller au cinéma/de faire du vélo**
I (don't) feel like going to the cinema/riding a bike

**je préfère** + the name of the activity you prefer doing

**je préfère rester à la maison/écouter de la musique/le ski**
I prefer to stay at home/to listen to music/to go skiing

---

**12. Say in French:**

1. In my free time, I like going to the theatre and going to the gym.
2. Tomorrow I'd like to go jogging. In the evening I'd like to eat out.
3. I don't feel like going to the beach and sunbathing, I prefer to go to the pool.
4. I don't like sport very much. In my free time I prefer to watch TV and surf the net.

---

**check your answers at**
www.collinslanguage.com/revolution

# 12 Unité douze
# Les vacances

## Hébergement Accommodation

**Green**
for go ahead

 56

Listen to the green words being pronounced and repeat them, thinking of their meaning as you do.

l'agence (f.) de voyage  travel agent
l'appartement (m.)  flat, apartment
la basse saison  low season
le B&B  B&B
le camping  camping
le camping-car  camper van
la caravane  caravan
l'excursion (f.)  excursion
la haute saison  high season
l'hôtel (m.)  hotel
la personne  person
la réservation  booking, reservation
la tente  tent
l'office (m.) du tourisme  tourist office
la villa  villa
le village touristique  tourist village
la visite guidée  guided visit
la vue  view

**Amber**
for wait
and think

 57

Listen to the amber and red words being pronounced and repeat them, visualising your links and images as you do.

la chambre simple  single room
la chambre double  double room
la chambre d'hôte  B&B
la climatisation  air conditioning
compris  included
la nuit  night
le petit-déjeuner  breakfast
le repas  meal
le tarif réduit  reduced rate

### How to remember amber words:

| | |
|---|---|
| **chambre** | Think of *chamber* and just switch the last two letters around. It can be a hotel room or a bedroom – both places you sleep. |
| **climatisation** | think of *climate* – with the air con' you have a nice *climate* in your room |
| **hôte** | think of *host* – B&Bs always have a host because they're in someone's house |

| | |
|---|---|
| **compris** | think of *compre*hensive: if something is comprehensive, it includes everything |
| **nuit** | tonight is the *new eve* of something great |
| **petit-déjeuner** | it's rather *petty* to write about your breakfast in a *daily journa*l |
| **repas** | we sometimes call a meal a repast |
| **tarif réduit** | think of *reduced tariff*, another expression for special rate |

**Red**
for stop, think, make a link

**l'auberge (f.) de jeunesse**  youth hostel
**la clé**  key
**la demi-pension**  half board
**la douche**  shower
**le gîte**  holiday cottage/self-catering accommodation
**le lit**  bed
**la pension complète**  full board
**la piscine**  swimming pool
**la salle de bains**  bathroom

### To help you memorise red words:

| | |
|---|---|
| **auberge de jeunesse** | your first meal at the youth hostel: *auberg*ine with a French *je-ne*-sais-quoi |
| **clé** | think of trying to open a door with a *clay* key – it will break in the lock! |
| **douche** | *do sh*ampoo and flowers go together in the shower? No! |
| **gîte** | imagine someone called Man*jeet* who rents self-catering accommodation for his holidays |
| **lit** | time for *Lee* to go to bed! |
| **pension complète** | think of being on a *pension* with a full board package |
| **piscine** | imagine yourself on holiday and trying to get some *peace in* the swimming-pool, floating on a comfortable airbed |
| **salle de bains** | the dog *Sal* is *ban*ned from the bathroom |

## Activités de mémorisation
### Memorising activities

**1. Select the words below that refer to des vacances à l'hôtel (a holiday in a hotel):**

chambre d'hôte   excursion   petit-déjeuner   salle de bains
climatisation   vue   clé   pension complète   gîte   réservation
auberge de jeunesse   douche   demi-pension   tarif réduit

1. ..............................          6. ..............................
2. ..............................          7. ..............................
3. ..............................          8. ..............................
4. ..............................          9. ..............................
5. ..............................          10. ..............................

**2. Match each beginning with its correct ending to make words related to holidays:**

1. l'aub- de jeun-              a. -ping-car
2. le gî-                       b. -tement
3. com-                        c. -erge  -esse
4. le cam-                      d. -te
5. l'appar-                     e. -pris

**3. Solve the anagrams of these four words related to holidays:**

1. PITTE -NUJEREDE          3. PIMGACN

2. VRACAANE                 4. TEIG

**4. Add the missing letters to make four places you may go to during a holiday.**

1. __ U __ __ __ __ __   __ __ __   __ __ __ __ __ __ S __ __

2. __ __ F __ __ __ __   __ __ __   __ __ __ __ R __ __ __ __

3. _ _ _ _ L _ _ _ _   _ _ _ _ R _ _ _ _ _ _ _

4. _ _ _ S _ _ _ _ _   _ _ _ _ _ _ _ E

**5. Complete the crossword puzzle below:**

**Across:**

1. night
3. flat, appartment
6. person
9. bed
10. key

**Down:**

2. shower
4. self-catering accommodation
5. season
7. meal
8. tent
10. air-conditioning
11. swimming-pool

**Green**
for go ahead

 58

Listen to the green and amber words being pronounced and repeat them, visualising your links as you do.

# Objets utiles pour les vacances Useful items to take on holiday

**la carte de crédit**  credit card
**la crème antiseptique**  antiseptic cream
**la crème solaire**  sun cream
**le passeport**  passport
**les sandales (f.)**  sandals
**le shampooing**  shampoo
**le chèque de voyage**  traveller's cheque

**les affaires (f.) de toilette**  toiletries
**l'après-soleil (m.)**  aftersun

**Amber**
for wait
and think

l'assurance (f.)  insurance
les bagages (m.) à main  hand luggage
la brosse  hairbrush
la brosse à dents  toothbrush
la carte  map
le dentifrice  toothpaste
les lunettes (f.) de soleil  sunglasses
la monnaie  coins, small change, currency
le permis de conduire  driver's licence
le sac de couchage  sleeping bag
la serviette  towel
les vêtements (m.)  clothes

**How to remember amber words:**

| | |
|---|---|
| **affaires de toilette** | imagine someone minding other people's *affairs* and asking questions about their *toilet*ries |
| **après-soleil** | think of *solar* and *après*-ski. On a sunny skiing day, you'll need some aftersun lotion. |
| **assurance** | insurance gives you *assurance* |
| **bagages à main** | link it with *baggage* and *mani*pulate |
| **brosse** | think of *bro's* brush |
| **brosse à dents** | think of your *dent*ist's *bro's* brush |
| **carte** | think of a small *cart* with a map on it |
| **dentifrice** | think of going to the *dent*ist for a check up and asking her to use *freez*ing toothpaste to polish your teeth |
| **lunettes de soleil** | link it with *solar* and imagine someone called *Lynette* wearing sunglasses |
| **monnaie** | link it with *mone*tary |
| **permis de conduire** | think of a bus *conduc*tor who's got *permis*sion to drive |

| | |
|---|---|
| **sac de couchage** | imagine a *sack* in which you feel as comfortable as on a *couch* |
| **serviette** | imagine trying to dry yourself after a bath with a table napkin! In French a serviette is a bath towel |
| **vêtements** | link it with *vestments* |

**l'appareil (m.) photo**  camera
**l'argent (m.)**  money
**le couteau suisse**  Swiss army knife
**le maillot de bain**  swimming costume
**le pansement**  plaster
**le sac à dos**  rucksack
**le savon**  soap
**la valise**  suitcase

**Red**
for stop, think,
make a link

 59

Listen to the red words being pronounced and repeat them, visualising your images as you do.

**To help you memorise red words:**

| | |
|---|---|
| **appareil photo** | imagine taking out your camera on a nice *April* day for some *April photos* |
| **argent** | you need a lot of money to fly to *Argent*ina |
| **maillot** | people don't want to look as white as *mayo*nnaise in their swim suit! |
| **pansement** | If you tried to make a *pan* out of *cement*, you might need a plaster |
| **sac à dos** | imagine carrying a ruck*sack* full of *dough* |
| **savon** | since working in cosmetics, he's got much more *savvy on* soap! |
| **valise** | imagine going through many *valleys* looking for your suitcase |

**Tony's Tip**

**Say it aloud!**
Every time you learn something new, say it aloud and keep repeating it until you can say it from memory, while imagining yourself in the situation being described. Not only will this help you to remember new words or expressions, it will also increase your confidence and your sense of being in control.

## Activités de mémorisation
Memorising activities

### 6. Match each French word or expression below with the correct picture:

a ................... b ................... c ................... d ...................

e ................... f ................... g ................... h ...................

sac de couchage    brosse à dents    couteau suisse    vêtements    savon

### 7. Complete the expressions using the endings below:

-reil  -ac  -dit  -se  -rance  -mis  -port  -te  -aires  -uire  -ès
-ette  -to  -leil  -os

1. carte de cré-
2. assu-
3. vali-
4. passe-
5. appa-  pho-

6. apr-  so-
7. aff-  de  toil-
8. per-  de  cond-
9. car-
10. s-  à d-

### 8. Add the missing letters to make four items to take on holiday:

1. __ R __ __ __ __ __

2. __ __ I __ __ __ __ __    __ __ B __ __ __

3. __ __ __ __ T __ __ __ __    __ __ __    __ __ __ __ __ I __

4. __ __ __ V __ __ __ __ __

# Allons un peu plus loin
## Let's go a bit further

When talking about holidays, the following expressions will be useful:

**par nuit/par personne** per night/per person

**(n')est (pas) compris** is (not) included

**en supplément** extra, not included

**tout compris** everything included

**petit-déjeuner compris** including breakfast

**repas compris** meals included

**combien coûte ...?** How much does ... cost?

**la douche/la clim(atisation)/le téléphone ne fonctionne pas**
the shower / the air conditioning/the telephone doesn't work

**il (n') y a (pas) d'eau chaude/de serviette/de papier toilette**
there is (no) hot water/a towel/toilet paper

**où est le parking/l'office du tourisme/la plage/le
restaurant/l'ascenseur?**
where is the car park/the tourist office/the beach/the restaurant/the lift?

 60

**9. Listen to the conversation between Annie and the hotel
receptionist and complete the table:**

| Type of room | |
|---|---|
| Number of nights | |
| Breakfast | |

**10. Say in French:**

1. I would like a single room with a shower for six nights.
2. How much is full board?
3. Is there a guided tour tomorrow?
4. Is there a reduced price for children?

**go to
www.collinslanguage.com/revolution
for extra activities**

## Chez moi At my place

**Green**
for go ahead

 61

Listen to the green words being pronounced and repeat them, thinking of their meaning as you do.

l'appartement (m.) flat, apartment
le balcon balcony
le garage garage
le parking parking, car park
le salon sitting room
la terrasse terrace
la villa detached house, villa

l'ascenseur (m.) lift
le bureau study
la chambre bedroom
la clim(atisation) air conditioning
la cuisine kitchen
l'entrée (f.) entrance hall
le jardin garden

**Amber**
for wait and think

 62

Listen to the amber and red words being pronounced and repeat them, visualising your links and images as you do.

### How to remember amber words:

| | |
|---|---|
| **ascenseur** | think of *ascending*, which means to go up |
| **bureau** | think of the beautiful old-fashioned desk, or 'bureau', which you would love to have in your study |
| **chambre** | you learned chambre in Unit 12. It's a hotel room and a bedroom – think of *chamber* |
| **climatisation** | think of *climate*, with the air con' you have a nice *climate* in your room |
| **cuisine** | think of cooking French *cuisine* in your kitchen |
| **entrée** | an entrance would not have 'No *entry*' written on it! |
| **jardin** | think of filling your garden with *jardini*ères, big pots of flowers |

**Red**
for stop, think,
make a link

**le chauffage** heating
**l'étage (m.)** floor, storey
**le rez-de-chaussée** ground floor
**la salle de bains** bathroom
**la salle à manger** dining room

**To help you memorise red words:**

**chauffage**    imagine your heating isn't working so you
go to a *show* about *far sh*ores where it's
always warm!

**étage**    Scarl*ett* has a gar*age* on the first floor

**rez-de-chaussée**    you might make a *reso*lution to *show* Say*ra*
the ground floor of your new house

**salle de bains**    remember *Sal* the dog from Unit 2? She was
*ban*ned from the bathroom for stealing the
toilet paper!

**salle à manger**    think of *Sal* the dog eating dinner from a
*manger* in the dining room

To talk about your house, you will need the following structures:

**c'est** + type of house/location/characteristics

**c'est un appartement/une villa/au premier étage/à la
campagne/grand**
it's a flat/a detached house/on the first floor/in the countryside/large

**il (n')y a (pas de)** + name of room or feature

**il y a un bureau/une salle à manger/trois chambres/deux
salles de bains/une piscine**
there is a study/a dining room/three bedrooms/two bathrooms/a
swimming pool

**il n'y a pas d'ascenseur/de jardin/de garage**
there is no lift/garden/garage

## Activités de mémorisation
Memorising activities

**1. Join the French words on the left to their correct English meaning on the right:**

| | | | |
|---|---|---|---|
| 1. | ascenseur | a. | flat |
| 2. | cuisine | b. | balcony |
| 3. | garage | c. | dining room |
| 4. | étage | d. | garden |
| 5. | chauffage | e. | lift |
| 6. | terrasse | f. | kitchen |
| 7. | appartement | g. | entrance hall |
| 8. | salle de bains | h. | garage |
| 9. | salon | i. | heating |
| 10. | jardin | j. | study |
| 11. | parking | k. | sitting room |
| 12. | bureau | l. | parking space |
| 13. | balcon | m. | bathroom |
| 14. | entrée | n. | terrace |
| 15. | salle à manger | o. | floor |

**2. Match each beginning with its correct ending to make the names of features in a house:**

| | | | |
|---|---|---|---|
| 1. | l'ascen | a. | rdin |
| 2. | le par | b. | sse |
| 3. | le ja | c. | atisation |
| 4. | la terra | d. | rage |
| 5. | le chauf | e. | on |
| 6. | la clim | f. | seur |
| 7. | le ga | g. | fage |
| 8. | le balc | h. | king |

**3. Solve the anagrams of these names of rooms:**

| | | | |
|---|---|---|---|
| 1. | LANOS | 3. | BLAI SA NEDLES |
| 2. | ICESUNI | 4. | RUUBAE |

**4. Add the missing letters to make four names of external features in a house:**

1. __ a __ __ __ __ __

3. __ __ __ a __ __

2. __ a __ __ __ __ __

4. __ __ r __ __ __ __ __ __

**5. Label each room in the picture with its name:**

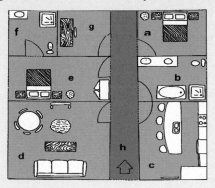

a. ...................    b. ...................    c. ...................    d. ...................

e. ...................    f. ...................    g. ...................    h. ...................

# **Les meubles** Furnishings

**Green**
for go ahead

 63

Listen to the green and amber words being pronounced and repeat them.

**Amber**
for wait
and think

**le bidet** bidet
**la lampe** lamp
**le miroir** mirror
**la table** table
**les toilettes (f.)** toilet

**le canapé** sofa
**la chaise** chair
**la cheminée** fireplace
**la commode** chest of drawers
**la cuisinière** cooker
**le frigo** fridge
**le lavabo** washbasin
**la machine à laver** washing machine

**How to remember amber words:**

| | |
|---|---|
| **canapé** | imagine a prawn *canapé* where the prawn is reclining comfortably on a *sofa* of bread or pastry |
| **chaise** | almost like chair, just swap **r** for **se** |
| **cheminée** | imagine Mary Poppins singing "Chim *chiminee*' when landing in the fire place |
| **commode** | a really big chest of drawers would be *commod*ious, but we also sometimes call a small chest of drawers a *commode* |
| **cuisinière** | French *cuisine? yeah!* on your new cooker! |
| **frigo** | imagine talking to a bottle of milk: "you're *free, go* to the fridge now!" |
| **lavabo, machine à laver** | link with *lavatory*, the old-fashioned word for the place where people washed |

**Red**
for stop, think,
make a link

 64

Listen to the red words being pronounced and repeat them, visualising your images as you do.

**l'armoire (f.)** wardrobe
**la baignoire** bath tub
**la douche** shower
**le fauteuil** armchair
**le four** oven
**le four à micro-ondes** microwave oven
**le lave-vaisselle** dishwasher
**le lit** bed
**la table de nuit** bedside cabinet

**To help you memorise red words:**

| | |
|---|---|
| **armoire** | originally, this was a cupboard for weapons, an *armoury*; so think of a wardrobe full of weapons |
| **baignoire** | imagine your *bête noire* in your bath! |
| **douche** | can you remember this from Unit 12? If not, go back and check |

| **fauteuil** | imagine sitting on a *faux*-leather armchair wearing a *tie* |
|---|---|
| **four** | think how much you could cook in a *four*-door oven! |
| **lave-vaisselle** | *sell* your dishwasher and be greener! c'est *la vie sell* |
| **lit** | Here's another you should be able to remember from Unit 12 – it was time for *Lee* go to bed! |
| **table de nuit** | think of a table for your night-time *need*s |

## Activités de mémorisation
### Memorising activities

**6. Put the items below into the room they normally go in:**

armoire   cheminée   canapé   table de nuit   table   commode   chaise
four   frigo   lavabo   cuisinière   machine à laver   miroir   lit
lave-vaisselle   fauteuil   douche

| Cuisine | Salon | Salle de bains | Chambre | Salle à manger |
|---|---|---|---|---|
| 1. ............ | ............ | ............ | ............ | ............ |
| 2. ............ | ............ | ............ | ............ | ............ |
| 3. ............ | ............ | ............ | ............ | |
| 4. ............ | | ............ | ............ | |
| 5. ............ | | ............ | | |

**7. Complete the words using the beginnings below:**

mach-   comm-   faut-   fri-   chem-   lave-vai-   ta-   table d-
arm-   cuis-

1. –e nuit
2. -euil
3. -ode
4. -oire
5. –ine à laver
6. -sselle
7. –ble
8. –inée
9. –inière
10. -go

**8. Add the missing letters to make four words for items found in a *chambre*:**

1. ___ ___ m ___ ___         3. ___ ___ t

2. ___ ___ m ___ ___ ___ ___    4. ___ ___ b ___ ___   ___ ___   ___ ___ ___ ___ ___

**9. Add the missing letters to make four words for items found in a *salle de bains*:**

1. ___ ___ ___ ___ ___ o

2. ___ ___ ___ ___ ___ t ___ ___ ___

3. ___ ___ r ___ ___ ___

4. ___ o ___ ___ ___ ___

65

**10. Listen to the conversation, then choose the correct answers:**

The house is:

a. in France
b. in England
c. very large
d. pretty
e. a one-storey building
f. a two-storey building

The house has:

g. one bedroom downstairs
h. one bedroom upstairs
i. two bathrooms
j. no garage
k. no garden

## Allons un peu plus loin
Let's go a bit further

To say what material or substance items are made of, you will need the following structure:

**C'est en** + name of the material

**Cet objet est en bois/métal/plastique/tissu/papier/cuir/ céramique/marbre/émail**
This object is made of wood/metal/plastic/fabric/paper/leather/ceramic/ marble/enamel

You can also extend what you've learnt in this unit by adding some of the words and expressions you've learnt in Unit 4 (Shapes, sizes and appearance) and Unit 5 (Clothes and colours).

**11. Give the English for the following:**

a. La table est rectangulaire, et fait un mètre quatre-vingts de long et quatre-vingts centimètres de large. Elle est en plastique rouge cerise, avec des pieds en métal gris.

b. Florence a un très beau nouveau canapé en cuir marron. Il n'est pas très grand, mais il est confortable!

c. C'est une armoire ancienne en bois léger avec des décorations en céramique bleue.

d. J'ai une cuisine très moderne, avec un frigo noir métallisé et des meubles jaunes.

**12. Say in French:**

a. The fireplace is made of white marble, with small decorations in cherry red enamel.

b. The second bedroom is rather small, only 4 square metres, but the furniture is pretty and light pink.

c. The bedroom is circular, over 4 metres in diameter. The bed is round, too: it is made of fabric and wood and is light brown.

## Pour finir: Mind Map it!

To exercise your memory, draw a Mind Map of your home.

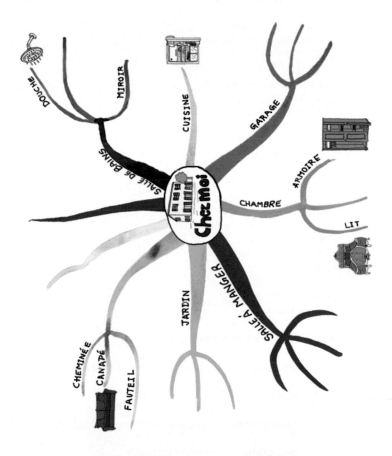

# L'informatique et les médias

## L'informatique Information technology

**Green**
for go ahead

 66

Listen to the green words being pronounced and repeat them, thinking of their meaning as you do.

l'adresse (f.) address
le café internet Internet café
le CD CD
cliquer to click
la connexion connection
le document document
l'e-mail (m.) e-mail
favoris favourites
formater to format
l'icone (f.) icon
insérer insert
le message message
la page web web page
le programme program

**Amber**
for wait and think

 67

Listen to the amber and red words being pronounced and repeat them, visualising your links and images as you do.

enregistrer save
deux points colon
le point dot
la recherche search
sélectionner select
sauvegarder save

### How to remember amber words:

| | |
|---|---|
| **enregistrer** | think of *register*, information is saved in *registers* |
| **point** | a point is a dot |
| **deux points** | you need two dots or *points* to make a colon |
| **recherche** | think of *research* |
| **sélectionner** | think of *selection* |
| **sauvegarder** | saving your documents will safe*guard* them |

**Red**
for stop, think,
make a link

**l'arobase (f.) (m.)**  at, @
**la barre oblique**  slash
**le clavier**  keyboard
**la clé USB**  memory stick, USB key
**le disque dur**  hard disk
**l'écran (m.)**  screen, monitor

**envoyer**  to send
**l'imprimante (f.)**  printer
**l'ordinateur (m.)**  computer
**la souris**  mouse
**le tiret**  dash, hyphen
**le tiret bas**  underscore

**To help you memorise red words:**

| | |
|---|---|
| **arobase** | picture a ballet dancer doing an *arabes*que with her leg coiled up in the shape of an @ |
| **barre oblique** | visualise an *oblique* metal *bar*, looking like a slash |
| **clavier** | imagine someone at the keyboard wearing a bala*clava* |
| **clé USB** | think of putting a *clay* USB key into your computer – not a good idea! |
| **disque dur** | think of *disc dur*ation as the amount of memory discs have – hard drives have much more memory space than floppy discs |
| **écran** | imagine a *cran*berry on your monitor as wallpaper |
| **envoyer** | *envoy*s take important messages from one government to another |
| **imprimante** | *imprint* is a printing term – imagine printing a book about *ants* on your new printer |
| **ordinateur** | think of a *co-ordinator* working on his/her computer |
| **souris** | *sorry*, I have been using your mouse |
| **tiret** | imagine a pre*tty ray* of sunshine darting across the window pane in the form of a dash or underscore |

## Activités de mémorisation
Memorising activities

**1. Join the French words on the left to their English meaning on the right:**

| | | | |
|---|---|---|---|
| 1. | arobase | a. | insert |
| 2. | connexion | b. | address |
| 3. | cliquer | c. | printer |
| 4. | enregistrer | d. | screen, monitor |
| 5. | écran | e. | underscore |
| 6. | insérer | f. | colon |
| 7. | imprimante | g. | send |
| 8. | adresse | h. | format |
| 9. | clavier | i. | slash |
| 10. | envoyer | j. | @ |
| 11. | tiret | k. | save |
| 12. | barre oblique | l. | connection |
| 13. | deux points | m. | save |
| 14. | tiret bas | n. | keyboard |
| 15. | formater | o. | dash |
| 16. | sauvegarder | p. | click |

**2. Match each beginning with its ending to make words related to IT:**

| | | | |
|---|---|---|---|
| 1. | l'e-m | a. | ne |
| 2. | le pro | b. | ment |
| 3. | le messa | c. | ctionner |
| 4. | l'ico | d. | voris |
| 5. | le docu | e. | erche |
| 6. | séle | f. | gramme |
| 7. | fav | g. | ail |
| 8. | la rech | h. | ge |

**3. Solve the anagrams of these IT-related words:**

| | | | |
|---|---|---|---|
| 1. | FACE REENTINT | 3. | GEAP EBW |
| 2. | SIQEDU URD | 4. | RISUSO |

### 4. Add the missing letters to make four IT-related actions:

1. __ n __ __ __ __ __

2. __ u __ __ __ __

3. __ __ __ q __ __ __

4. __ __ s __ __ __ __ __

### 5. Write the correct French word under the picture:

a. ..................... b. ..................... c. ..................... d. .....................

e. ..................... f. ..................... g. ..................... h. .....................

### 6. Complete the crossword puzzle with IT-related words:

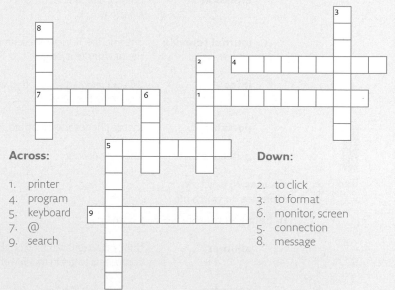

**Across:**

1. printer
4. program
5. keyboard
7. @
9. search

**Down:**

2. to click
3. to format
6. monitor, screen
5. connection
8. message

## Les médias The media

l'article (m.) article
la carte téléphonique phone card
le documentaire documentary
le journal newspaper
le magazine magazine
le mobile mobile phone
la presse press

la radio radio
la station station
la télé(vision) television
le téléphone telephone

la chaîne channel
l'émission (f.) broadcast
le journal télé(visé) TV news programme
les info(rmations) (f.) news
le portable mobile phone, laptop
la publicité advertising

**Green**
for go ahead

68

Listen to the green words being pronounced and repeat them, thinking of the meaning or visualising your links as you do.

**Amber**
for wait
and think

**How to remember amber words:**

| | |
|---|---|
| **chaîne** | think of learning about a *chain* reaction on the news channels |
| **émission** | think of a broadcast on greenhouse gas *emission*s |
| **journal télévisé** | imagine the TV news presenter reading out the news from a *journal* |
| **infos** | think of *information*, another way of describing the news |
| **portable** | mobile phones and laptop are *portable* devices |
| **publicité** | think of *publicity* |

**Red**
for stop, think,
make a link

allumer to switch on
éteindre to switch off

69

Listen to the amber and red words being pronounced and repeat them, visualising your images as you do.

**To help you memorise red words:**

| | |
|---|---|
| **allumer** | think of *alumni* switching on their computers to get in touch with each other |
| **éteindre** | imagine a child having *a tantru*m when you switch off the TV |

**Tony's Tip**

**Use your whole brain!**
We all need to use both sides of our brain to maximise our learning abilities. While studying, your left brain is working hard on words, sentences and logic. Your creative right brain kicks into action when you are relaxing – and this is the time to review your visualisations and come up with new ones that work better for you. Involve your right brain by Mind Mapping, drawing pictures, listening to music and singing songs.

## Activités de mémorisation
### Memorising activities

**7. List the items below according to the type of communication they refer to: la presse, la télévision or les communications téléphoniques**

magazine   chaîne   article   documentaire   journal télé   émission
mobile   carte téléphonique   station   infos   publicité   journal
téléphone   portable

| Presse | Télévision | Communications téléphoniques |
|--------|------------|------------------------------|
| 1. .................. | .................. | .................. |
| 2. .................. | .................. | .................. |
| 3. .................. | .................. | .................. |
| 4. .................. | .................. | .................. |
| 5. .................. | .................. | |
| 6. | .................. | |
| 7. | .................. | |

**8. Complete the words using the endings below:**

-nal   -ntaire   -tion   -sion   -ndre   -cle   -fos   -azine   -dio
-lé   -umer   -al

1. docume-
2. étei-
3. jour-
4. té-
5. sta-
6. all-

7. arti-
8. mag-
9. journ-
10. émis-
11. ra-
12. in-

**9. Add the missing letters to make four words related to TV:**

1. ___ ___ ___ ___ ___ c ___ ___ ___

2. ___ h ___ ___ ___ ___

3. ___ ___ ___ ___ m ___ ___

4. ___ ___ e ___ ___ ___ ___ ___

**10. Add the missing letters to make four words related to the press:**

1. ___ ___ ___ ___ c ___ ___

2. ___ ___ g ___ ___ ___ ___ ___

3. ___ ___ u ___ ___ ___ ___

4. ___ n ___ ___ ___

**11. Listen to the conversation, then complete with the missing information:**

a. l'adresse email de Jacques est ..................................

b. la page web du magasin l'Epicerie est ..............................

c. le numéro de portable de Julie est ..................................

# Allons un peu plus loin
## Let's go a bit further

The following structures will be useful when dealing with telephones and computers:

**Puis-je** + the action you would like to perform

**Puis-je envoyer un email/utiliser cet ordinateur/sauvegarder un document/imprimer un document?**
Can I send a message/use this computer/save a document/print a document?

**Je voudrais** + item you would like or action you would like to perform

**Je voudrais une carte téléphonique/un journal en anglais/ regarder une chaîne anglophone**
I would like a phone card/an English newspaper/to watch an English speaking channel

---

**12. Say in French:**

a.  Can I switch on the television?

b.  I would like to send this document.

c.  I would like to send an e-mail.

d.  Can I use this printer?

**go to**
www.collinslanguage.com/revolution
**for extra activities**

# Don't forget ... more fantastic titles in the Collins Language Revolution range:

**To order in the UK**
call 0845 241 9972

**To order outside the UK**
call +44 (0) 870787 1732

£19.99 **Language Revolution Beginner**
French 978-0-00-725594-8
Italian 978-0-00-725511-5
Spanish 978-0-00-725535-1

£22.50 **Language Revolution Beginner Plus**
French 978-0-00-725595-5
Italian 978-0-00-725512-2
Spanish 978-0-00-725536-8

£34.99 **Language Revolution Complete Pack**
French 978-0-00-732116-2
Italian 978-0-00-732117-9
Spanish 978-0-00-732118-6

And for your dictionary ...

£8.99 **Collins Easy Learning French Dictionary**
978-0-00-725349-4

£9.99 **Collins Easy Learning Italian Dictionary**
978-0-00-726106-2

£8.99 **Collins Easy Learning Spanish Dictionary**
978-0-00-725350-0